Erb Family Cookbook

Theresa (Erb) Henderson

Erbs & Spices Family Cookbook

A Companion To the Growing Erbs Series

Illustrated by
Rozanne (Erb) Koski

Erb Family Cookbook

ERBS & SPICES FAMILY COOKBOOK
Copyright © 2004 by Theresa Henderson
Illustrations Copyright © 2004 by Rozanne Koski
Printed in the United States of America. All rights reserved,
including the right of reproduction in whole or in part in any form.

Erb Family Cookbook
~Dedication~

I dedicate this family cookbook to my sister, Sheila Caza, author of "The Growing Erbs Series".
Reading her stories inspired me to compile these great family recipes.
Thanks, Sheila, for bringing all those memories to life again and for preserving our family history into such a wonderful keepsake.

Sheila & Theresa (1977)

Dedication, con't

Sheila & Rozanne

Rozanne, Sheila, Theresa

Rozanne, Sheila, Diane

Kimberly & Sheila

Sheila & Paul

Erb Family Cookbook

Thank You

to all the contributors of this cookbook:
To Grandma Erb,
who was a great cook and passed that love on;
To Aunt Anna,
who had many of Grandma Erb's recipes,
(some in Grandma's own handwriting);
To my sisters and sister-in-law,
Who shared their favorite recipes;
And to Mom,
who took the time to go through her recipes.
helping me find the ones I needed for this book,
and for teaching me how to cook!

The stories in this book are all *based* on real events even though I had to add a certain amount of fiction as I could not remember every detail.

However, the recipes are all real…

Erb Family Cookbook

CONTENTS:

Recipes:

Appetizers	16
Bars	18
Beverages	32
Breads	33
Breakfast Dishes	41
Cakes & Frostings	48
Candy	66
Canning & Preserving	74
Cookies	87
Desserts	110
Main Courses	124
Pies	141
Salads	161
Soups	170
Vegetables	175
Index	189

Stories:

Bonanza	84
Closet Treasure	12
Company's Coming & Dad's Cooking!	153
Diane's Taffy Pull	178
Dear Grandma Letter	121
Family (Poem)	188
Grandma & Grandpa Oswald	26
My First Cooking Experience	46
Paul Cooks	62
To Grandmother's House We Go	133

Erb Family Cookbook
A note from the author…

Growing up in the 1960's was a special time. I wasn't aware of the world's problems. I was only concerned about my little world, which actually seemed pretty big at the time. Our parents were from the German Mennonite heritage. That meant to me, that they were good cooks and that God was as much a part of their lives as the air they breathed. There was never an extended family gathering that did not include good food and a lively discussion of the Bible. Fortunately for the kids, the discussion followed the food, so we were able to slip away and play, thus avoiding the friendly interchange that often caused raised voices.

It doesn't seem that you can write about our family without including some of the wonderful recipes that were a part of our life together. Following you will find many family recipes interspersed with little stories. I hope you'll find some of them as special as we do when we remember them from our youth.

Theresa Henderson

Grandma Erb, reading her Bible
with her "devotional covering" on.
(A little cap that Mennonite women wear.)

Erb Family Cookbook
Closet Treasure

Somehow Theresa had managed to find an almost empty bag of brown sugar during the move to the farm. She was sure Mom wouldn't care if she "got rid of it" so she discreetly took it upstairs to the bedroom. Looking around the room she shared with her two sisters, Rozanne and Sheila, she decided there wasn't enough for all three, so to save them the disappointment of not getting a share, she decided to hide the golden brown treasure in a safe place to be eaten later when she was alone. Everything in the room was rather every which way. The bed frames were set up, yet the mattresses waited along one wall for someone to lay them down for a rest. The dresser was in the middle of the room with boxes stacked along a far wall. Well, this room wasn't looking like a place to hide anything. Everything was still out of place, which meant that someone would be going through things soon. Maybe Diane's room would have a spot to bury a treasure.

As you came upstairs, there were three rooms that lay before you. On the right was the room that would belong to "the three little girls". In the middle, Paul, the only brother, had his room. And to the left was the room that belonged to Theresa's oldest sister, Diane. At 13, Diane was so grown-up. Theresa was just enthralled with her oldest sister. She was kind and quiet and so smart. And, missing from her room at the moment. In fact, the whole upstairs was empty. Hence, a good time for hiding her sugary treat.

Diane's room was already more organized. Though the mattress was resting comfortably on the bed, the sheets and blankets had not yet covered its blue and white stripped pattern. The dresser was over by the wall, all filled with Diane's clothing. That looked like a safe place to tuck something away. Just as she reached the dresser, with one hand in mid-air, Theresa heard feet on the step. Oh no! For safety's sake, she thought she'd better hide. It might be Rose and Sheila after her stash!

Quickly she ran to Diane's closet, slipped into the lower back portion and held the nearly empty bag tightly in her clenched hands. She tried not to breathe, so no one would find her.

Steps went into Paul's room. There was a rummaging through some boxes and then the feet went back down the stairs. Theresa could smell the sweet fragrance of brown sugar through the opened end of her package. Maybe she'd better have a bite to sustain her. She carefully and quietly opened it. Dipping her hand inside, she pinched out a portion. That's the way to eat brown sugar, you know. Mom often let Theresa have a pinch as she stood on a chair watching her mix cookies. You have to clump it so it stays together and then once inside the mouth, its sweetness dissolves on the center of your tongue. Wow! Was that tasty! So sweet and grainy and smooth all in one...........

"What ya got there?"

Theresa looked up, surprised, and the most recent pinch of sugar wasn't pinched as tight, hence some fell to the closet floor. She hadn't heard Rozanne and Sheila come up the stairs and in the room. She'd been too enthralled with the sugar high. Dog-gone if they didn't always seem to know where she was!

"Just an old bag of brown sugar," she replied. "There's not hardly none left. Mom won't care." And then thinking quickly of a way to save her secrecy, "Want some?"

Sheila and Rose slipped into their rightful positions beside her and the bag was emptied in no time.

I wonder if a mouse found that sugar later and had a treat of its own...

RECIPE FOR CLOSET TREASURE
Ingredients:
1 nearly empty bag of light brown sugar
1 little girl with a sweet tooth
1 closet
Directions:
Add brown sugar to little girl. Put in closet. Enjoy!

Erb Family Cookbook

APPETIZERS

BUFFALO WINGS   Kim

3 lbs. Sectioned chicken wings/drumettes, broiled or baked until done
1 stick (½ cup) butter
1 oz Tabasco sauce (half of a small bottle)
Bleu cheese dressing & celery

Melt butter, add Tabasco, stir to mix, spoon glaze over hot chicken pieces. Serve with fresh celery sticks and dressing for dipping.

CHEESE BALL   Theresa

2 8 oz pkgs cream cheese
1 8 oz can crushed pineapple, drained
1 cup chopped pecans or walnuts
¼ cup green pepper, chopped fine
2 Tbsp onion, chopped fine
1 Tbsp seasoned salt

Soften cream cheese. Mix in other ingredients. Chill. Form into ball. Roll in more chopped nuts. Chill again.

DEVILLED EGGS   Theresa

12 eggs
½ cup Miracle Whip (may need more)
2 tsp mustard

Boil eggs for 10 minutes. Cool. Peel. Cut in half; scoop

yolk out and mash all yolks together. Mix with Miracle Whip and mustard. Salt to taste. Fill egg halves and sprinkle with seasoned salt.

PICKLE ROLL UPS   Theresa

Average sized dill pickles, halved
Thinly sliced pastrami (Budding or similar brand)
American cheese, cut to fit pickle halves
Place cheese on pickle and wrap with pastrami. Chill one hour or more.

WINGIES   Theresa

2 cups soy sauce
½ cup white sugar
½ cup oil
2 tsp garlic salt
2 cups water
¾ cup pineapple juice
2 tsp ginger
4 lbs. chicken wings (family packs)

Combine sauce; marinate wings overnight. Turn several times. Line jelly roll pan with foil (fills 2 sheets full). Fish wingies out of marinade with tongs and put on pans. Bake 350 degrees 1- 1 ½ hours or until golden brown.

BARS

BROWNIES   **Grandma Erb**

1 stick oleo
1 cup sugar
1 can Hershey's syrup (16 oz)
4 eggs, one at a time
1 cup flour
1 tsp vanilla
1 cup chopped pecans or walnuts

Cream sugar and oleo; add syrup, eggs, flour; mix well. Then add vanilla and nuts. Pour into a greased pan (9x13). Bake at 350 degrees for 25 minutes.

Frosting:
5 minutes before brownies are done, combine in saucepan:
¼ cup oleo
2 ½ Tbsp milk
¾ cup sugar

Bring to a boil and boil one minutes; stir in ¼ cup chocolate chips. Frost brownies as soon as they come out of the oven.

DATE BARS   **Grandma Erb**

Make a crumbly mixture of following:
1 cup shortening
1 cup brown sugar
2 cups flour
2 ½ cups oatmeal
1 tsp salt
½ tsp soda in 1 Tbsp water

Cook together and cool:
1 lb. dates, cut fine
1 cup water
1 cup sugar

Press ½ of mixture in greased pan, then put date mixture on top. Then rest of crumbly mixture. Bake at 350 degrees for 30 minutes. Cut in squares.

DATE & ORANGE SLICE BARS
Velma Hoffman

½ lb. dates
½ cup sugar
2 Tbsp flour
1 cup water
1 cup brown sugar
¾ cup shortening
2 eggs
1 tsp soda in 2 Tab hot water
1 tsp vanilla
1 ¾ cup flour
salt to taste
½ cup nuts
1 – 15 oz pkg orange slice candy

Combine first four ingredients in saucepan and cook until thick. Cool. Mix remaining ingredients except orange candy. Spread half of dough in greased 9x13 pan. Cover with orange slices, cut lengthwise in thirds. Spread date mixture over orange slices and top with remainder of batter. Bake at 350 degrees for 40 minutes. Cool and cut into bars.

GRAHAM CRACKER BARS   Mom

Put whole graham crackers on bottom of pan. Add filling:
1 cup brown sugar
1 cup crushed graham cracker crumbs
½ cup butter
½ cup milk
1 cup fine coconut
Boil five minutes. Cool. Spread on crackers and put more crackers on top. Frost with powder sugar icing.

GERMAN CHOCOLATE CARAMEL BARS
Theresa

1 German Chocolate Cake mix
1/3 cup evaporated milk
¾ cup melted butter
Mix together and bake 15 minutes. Remove from oven and drop pan so cake falls. Meanwhile, unwrap and melt 40 caramels and 1/3 cup evaporated milk. Pour over cake in pan. Sprinkle with one 12 oz package of milk chocolate chips (may use semi sweet) and chopped walnuts. Bake 15 minutes more.

LEMON BARS   Theresa

1 pkg one step angel food cake mix
1 can lemon pie filling

Mix together (by hand) the two ingredients. Put in greased jelly roll pan. Bake at 350 degrees 15-20 minutes or until done. Cool. Frost with powdered sugar and lemon juice mixed together.

MIXED NUT BARS   Mom

Crust:
1 ½ cup flour
¾ cup brown sugar
¼ tsp salt
½ cup soft oleo
Mix, press with fingers in a 9x13 inch pan. Bake at 350 degrees for 10 minutes. Cool. Spread on a can of mixed nuts.
Topping:
1 pkg (6 oz) butterscotch chips
½ cup light Karo syrup
2 Tbsp butter
Melt over low heat, pour over nuts. Bake 10 minutes more. Cool and cut.

PEANUT BUTTER BARS   Aunt Mabel

½ cup shortening
1 cup brown sugar
1 egg, beaten well and add
½ cup peanut butter
1 tsp vanilla
Add:
2 cups flour
½ tsp soda
½ tsp salt
Add:
½ cup oatmeal
Bake 350 degrees. Frost with powdered sugar peanut butter frosting or honey peanut butter frosting.

PUMPKIN BARS   Mom

4 eggs
1 cup salad oil
2 cups sugar
1 15 oz can pumpkin
Mix above ingredients in a large bowl. Sift the following and add to above. Stir.
2 cups flour
2 tsp baking powder
1 tsp soda
½ tsp salt
2 tsp cinnamon
½ tsp each ginger, cloves and nutmeg
Mix well and pour into greased and floured pan (12x18x1). Bake at 350 degrees for 25-30 minutes.

FROSTING:
6 oz cream cheese, softened
¾ stick butter
1 Tbsp cream or milk
1 tsp vanilla
4 cups powdered sugar
Beat cheese, butter, vanilla and cream until soft. Add powdered sugar until correct consistency to spread. Cut into 2"x 3" bars. Makes 36 bars. NOTE: pumpkin bars freeze well.

RAISIN BARS   Aunt Jeannie

1 cup raisins
1 cup sugar
1 cup water
2 Tbsp flour
Cook until thick. Set aside.
½ cup margarine

1 cup brown sugar
2 eggs
1 tsp soda
½ tsp salt
1 cup oatmeal
1½ cup flour

Put ½ in pan, then raisin mixture, then remaining ½. Bake ½ hour at 350 degrees.

RAISIN BARS   Mom

Boil 1 cup raisins and 2 cups water for 10 minutes.
Add: ½ cup butter while hot, then cool.
Sift and add to the above:
1¾ cup flour
1 tsp soda
½ tsp salt
1 cup sugar
½ tsp cinnamon
½ tsp cloves
½ tsp nutmeg

Pour in a 9x13 greased pan and bake 375 degrees approximately 30 minutes.

SALTED NUT ROLL BARS   Mom

Two -16 oz jars dry roasted peanut
Two -12 oz pkgs of peanut butter chips
6 Tbsp butter
Two - cans sweetened condensed milk
Two - 10 oz pkgs miniature marshmallows

In cookie sheet pan, pour 1 jar peanuts. Melt PB chips and butter. Mix together and add milk. Return to low heat and mix together well. Don't boil. Stir in marshmallows.

Spread on top of peanuts. Put other jar of peanuts on top. Press them down and cool.

7 LAYER BARS or MAGIC COOKIE BARS   Mom

Melt ¼ lb. Butter in an ungreased cake pan (9x 13). Sprinkle in order given:
1 cup graham cracker crumbs
6 oz pkg chocolate chips
6 oz pkg peanut butter or butterscotch chips
1 cup coconut
1 cup chopped nuts
1 can sweetened condensed milk
Bake 30 minutes at 350 degrees. Cool before cutting.

SUGARLESS BARS   Sue
(Sue's Mom's recipe & her Dad's favorite bars)

1 cup raisins
1 cup prunes (cut up)
1 cup dates (cut up)
2 cups water
Boil the above for 5 minutes. Take off stove and add two sticks of margarine or butter and let cool. When cooled, add:
2 tsp soda
2 cups flour
½ tsp salt
2 tsp cinnamon
1 tsp vanilla
Bake 25 minutes at 350 degrees in a greased 9x13 pan. May bake it in an 8"square pan if you want it thicker like cake.

TOFFEE SQUARES — **Mom**

1 cup butter or margarine
1 cup brown sugar
1 egg yolk
1 tsp vanilla
2 cups flour
½ tsp salt
1 cup chocolate chips
½ cup chopped nuts

Mix all but chips and nuts. Spread in a 9x13 pan (ungreased). Bake 25 minutes or until lightly browned, but not firm to touch. Melt chocolate chips over hot water and spread on cookie surface while warm. Sprinkle with nuts and cut into bars while warm.

YUMMY WHEATIES BARS — **Sheila**

1 ½ cup corn syrup
1 ½ cup sugar
2 Tbsp water

Cook over low heat. Stir constantly (3-5 minutes). Add 1 ½ cup peanut butter and 1 tsp vanilla. Add to: 4 cups or more Wheaties, and 1 ½ cups peanuts (less is using crunchy peanut butter). May also use sunflower seeds.
*In another recipe Sheila added 2 ½ cups crunchy peanut butter and 6 cups Wheaties, 2 tsp vanilla, (no peanuts) and raisins, if desired. Pour into cake pan or cookie sheet. Frost with chocolate if desired.

Erb Family Cookbook
Grandpa and Grandma Oswald

As the family car pulled down the shady street lined with tall oaks, the five children stretched and anxiously looked out the windows for their Grandparent's house. It was a late Sunday afternoon and they had been to visit their Aunt Verda and Uncle Jim on the farm. It had been an afternoon of good food and lots of playing. A trip from Park Rapids to Detroit Lakes on a Sunday was pretty common for the Erb Family and never passed without a visit to Grandma and Grandpa Oswald. They were Mom's parents and they lived in the town of Detroit Lakes. Their house was a pretty little yellow one with a great hill for rolling down in the back yard. There was a matching yellow garage that was rarely opened and the children always spent some time looking in the windows. It was perfectly spotless and very orderly and it was terribly hard to only look and not go in. But not too hard, as Grandma kept it locked tight.

As they pulled up to the curb outside the front of the house, Theresa spotted Grandpa's yellow car. It was sparkling clean and had wings out the back. Specifically it was a 1959 Rambler American, but Theresa didn't know that. It hardly looked used, although Grandpa used it regularly to go downtown. Theresa was glad that Grandpa was home. He loved the children and always had some special treat for them.

They went up the back step and Mom knocked on the door while everyone waited. The door opened and there was Grandpa's smiling face. His eyes even smiled, Theresa noticed. They all trooped into the house. It had a narrow dining room and kitchen all in one. It also had a peculiar smell to it. Theresa had never noticed other houses to have their own smell, except Uncle Jim's. It smelt like wood smoke. She couldn't quite identify the smell at her grandparent's house, but knew that it was partly from being closed up (she'd never seen a window open) and partly the smell left over from a meal.

Grandpa went to get Grandma from the other

room and soon came back. Grandma had been napping. Grandpa had a little radio he had been listening to the ballgame on, but he shut it off. Grandma came out then, her hair slightly mussed and she quickly set about heating water for a cup of instant coffee. Grandpa and Grandma always drank instant coffee. That was something the kids didn't see too often. Mom and Dad drank coffee from a coffeepot. The kids went outside to explore a bit and besides, the grown-up talk wasn't nearly as interesting as a hill for rolling and a garage that needed to be peeked at.

Grandma Oswald, Mom (in Grandma's kitchen)

After awhile, Mom called out the screen door that Grandpa had a treat. The kids traipsed back in and on the table were a box of Chicken in the Biscuit crackers and a bottle of Tang. Grandpa cheerfully passed the crackers around. They were a real treat because the only crackers the children got were soda or graham. These had a wonderful chicken flavor that just made you want to eat more and more, but Mom said only 5 each. Then Grandpa asked if anyone wanted a glass of Tang. Silly question, Theresa thought. Of course they did! Small glasses were set out and filled with water, then a spoonful of the dry powdered mix was added to each and stirred. Every child took a glass. It was sort of like orange juice only sweeter and smoother. And the water wasn't real cold, but it still tasted great to the kids. Grandma was telling Mom about the mending she was doing for Dale's kids. Dale was Mom's brother and he had so many kids, Theresa couldn't keep track of them all, but she was very fond of the oldest child, Shirley, who was actually an adult. Shirley was always nice to her and Theresa thought she was wonderful. Grandma did lots of mending for Dale's kids on her little treadle sewing machine. She had a pile of jeans laying there that she had been working on.

After the snack, the kids went into the living room and Grandma said they could play the organ if they kept the door shut and were quiet. They carefully opened the glass door between the kitchen and living room and all slipped inside. It was a wonderful place to look around. Referred to as "the front room" by Grandma, there was a flowered couch, a hairy rocker, and an overstuffed chair. A big rug covered the center of the floor. Diane played the organ first, while the younger kids looked at themselves in the oval mirror behind the chair, checked the little lamp that made the picture of the car look like it was moving when turned on and quietly explored Grandma's bedroom and the bathroom.

It wasn't long before Mom came in and said it was time to go. The children left the room through the front door with a little roof overhanging it and headed towards the car. Grandpa and Grandma came out to say good-bye and Theresa gave Grandpa a hug and remembered to thank him for the wonderful treats. She kissed his whiskered cheek as he bent down to tell her she was welcome and then they all piled into the car for the long drive home.

(Treats at Grandpa's included Tang, Chicken in a Biscuit crackers, Bugles, Limburger cheese, Braunsweiger meat, and onion and peanut butter sandwiches. Also, store bought cookies were occasionally set out.)

Grandpa & Grandma Oswald (at their home)

Theresa, Sheila & Grandpa Oswald in foreground
at Grandma & Grandpa's for dinner

BEVERAGES

HOT CHOCOLATE MIX   Rozanne

5 1/3 cups powdered dry milk
1- 1 lb. can Nestle's Quik (2 ½ cups)
1 cup powdered sugar
1 – 6 oz bottle Cremora or Coffee Mate

Mix all and store in airtight container. Use ¼ to 1/3 to 1 cup boiling water.

HOT CHOCOLATE MIX   Kim

4 cups powdered milk
1 lb-can Nestle Quik
1 cup powdered sugar
1 6-oz jar Cremora or Coffeemate

Mix all; store airtight.
Add 1/4-1/3 cup to 1 cup boiling water.

Dad, and Mom at Theresa's 1977 Graduation

BREADS

AMISH PUMPKIN BREAD — Mom

3 cups sugar
1 cup oil
1 lb. canned pumpkin
2/3 cup water
4 beaten eggs
3 ½ cups flour
2 tsp salt
2 tsp soda
1 tsp cinnamon
½ tsp cloves
1 tsp allspice
1 tsp nutmeg

Beat well and bake in greased and floured loaf pans one hour at 350 degrees.

BANANA NUT BREAD — Mom

Sift together and set aside:
2 cups flour
1 tsp baking powder
½ tsp soda
1 tsp salt
Cream well:
1 cup sugar
½ cup shortening
Blend in 2 eggs.
Stir in: 1 cup mashed bananas.
Blend in dry ingredients and add ½ cup chopped nuts.
Bake 350 degrees 60-70 minutes in greased loaf pan..

Mom, holding Annie (Rozanne's daughter)
Dad, holding Patrick & Shelly (Paul's children)

BANANA BREAD   Theresa

1 2/3 cup sugar
1 ¼ cups mashed bananas, (about 3 medium)
2/3 cup shortening
2/3 cup buttermilk
3 eggs
2 1/3 cups flour
1 ¼ tsp soda
1 ¼ tsp baking powder
1 tsp salt
2/3 cup chopped nuts, optional

Beat all until smooth. Pour into greased pans, 2 large or 4 small. Bake at 350 degrees 50 minutes or until done. Cool 10 minutes and remove from pans. Cool completely.

BLUBERRY MUFFINS — Mom

(From Val Chatel Ski Lodge Restaurant, where my Mom & Dad would go out for dinner at night and sometimes take us kids on Sunday for the Smorgasbord.)

2 cups sugar
4 eggs
2 cups milk
1 cup oil
Mix together with a fork and add:
6 cups flour
8 tsp baking powder
2 tsp salt
Fold in:
3 cups blueberries
Bake at 325 degrees for 15-17 minutes. Makes about 3 dozen.

Val Chatel Ski Lodge

CARAMEL ROLLS   Mom

Mom used whatever dough she had at the time. Even bread dough worked great. Roll out dough into rectangle. Butter. Sprinkle with brown sugar; over this sprinkle cinnamon. Roll up and cut. Place in greased 9x13 inch pan. Mix brown sugar and cream until smooth. Pour over rolls in pan. Let rise and bake until done. May put chopped pecans or walnuts on top before coving with caramel mixture. Mom sometimes put raisins in with the brown sugar and cinnamon before rolling up. When done, flip pan over to get rolls out.

DONUTS   Grandma Erb

4 cups flour
1 cup sugar
1 cup milk
¼ cup melted butter
5 tsp baking powder
1 tsp salt
½ tsp nutmeg
½ tsp cinnamon
2 eggs
1 tsp vanilla

Roll to 1/3 inch, cut, let stand 15 minutes, fry in hot deep fat at 375 degrees about 3 minutes, then turn over and brown.

EASY CARAMEL ROLLS   Rozanne

2 loaves frozen bread dough, thawed but not risen.
Cut lengthwise and then in half. Grease 9x13 pan. Arrange cuts in pan. Melt 1 stick oleo and 1 cup unpacked

brown sugar. Add 1 tsp cinnamon, 1 tsp vanilla and 1 pkg regular vanilla pudding (not instant).
Pour over dough. Let rise 1 hour. Bake 350 degrees for 35 minutes or until done.

LIGHT AND AIRY BUNS   **Theresa**

1 cup warm water
2 pkgs yeast
1 tsp sugar
½ cup melted shortening
3 ½ cups warm water
½ tsp butter flavoring
2 Tbsp vinegar
1 cup sugar
1 Tbsp salt
8-10 cups flour

Dissolve yeast in 1 cup water with 1 tsp sugar. Add remaining ingredients. Mix well and knead. Raise once, then shape and raise again. Bake on greased sheets 400 degrees about 10 minutes or until golden.

OVERNIGHT BUNS   **Grandma Erb**

Boil for 5 minutes:
1 ½ cups sugar
4 cups water.
Remove from stove and add 1 cup lard.
Let cool and add:
1 Tbsp salt
4 beaten eggs
1 pkg yeast, dissolved in ½ cup warm water
Flour, enough for a medium dough.
Set these buns at 2 pm. They will be ready to knead down

by 5 or 5:30. Shape into buns at bedtime, cover with cloth. Do not refrigerate. Bake in morning. Makes 4-5 dozen.

PEACHES AND CREAM MUFFINS   Theresa

2 cups canned peaches, drained (save juice)
4 cups flour
2 cups sugar
2 tsp baking powder
½ tsp salt
3 eggs
¾ cup oil
2 cups milk
Filling:
8 oz cream cheese, softened
¾ cup sugar
1 Tbsp reserved peach juice
1 tsp almond flavoring
Topping:
½ cup sugar
1 tsp cinnamon

Dice drained peaches to size of peas. Set aside. In bowl, mix flour, sugar, baking powder, and salt. Mix eggs and oil in separate bowl, then whisk in milk. Combine 2 mixtures. Fold in peaches. For filling: beat cream cheese, sugar, juice and almond. Fill greased muffin tins ½ full of batter. Drop 1 tsp filling into each. Top with 1 ½ Tbsp more batter. For topping: combine and sprinkle over muffins. Bake in preheated oven at 350 degrees approximately 20 minutes. Best served warm. Make 24.

ROLL DOUGH   Aunt Mabel

1 cup sugar
2 Tbsp salt
2 Tbsp shortening
4 cups boiling water
Bring these four ingredients to a boil. Let cool. Add:
2 tsp yeast which has been put into ½ cup warm water and
1 tsp sugar
When sugar water is lukewarm, add yeast and put in enough flour to make a soft sponge. Add 3 beaten eggs to sponge. Mix well and add enough flour to make a medium soft dough. Knead well and put in greased pan to rise. I use my big Tupperware dish with the lid. Let rise till full, punch down to let rise again and make into rolls, or buns or coffeecakes. Bake at 350 degrees till lightly brown.

Note from Theresa: I made 2 9x13 pans of cinnamon rolls and 2 loaves of bread.

RYE BREAD   Mom

1 1/8 cup warm water
2 Tbsp molasses
3 cups white flour
½ cup rye flour
3 Tbsp brown sugar
1 tsp salt
1 Tbsp shortening
1 ½ tsp yeast

Put in bread machine in order listed. Mix on dough setting. When done, take out and shape into loaf. Place in greased 9 inch loaf pan. Let rise until doubled. Bake at 350 degrees for 25 minutes. Remove from pan and cool. *Note: may mix and bake in bread machine. Use light setting.*

STRAWBERRY BUTTER   Kim

8 Tbsp unsalted butter
8 oz cream cheese
¼ to ½ cup powdered sugar
¼ tsp vanilla
12 large fresh strawberries, cleaned and hulled

Place all in food processor/blender, blend until smooth. Store airtight in refrigerator; bring to room temp before using. (Good on toast, bagels, etc.)

BREAKFAST DISHES

BEST BUTTERMILK PANCAKES — Theresa

1½ cup buttermilk
1 egg
2 Tbsp oil
1 Tbsp sugar
1 tsp vanilla
1 tsp butter flavoring
1¼ cup flour
1 tsp baking powder
½ tsp salt
½ tsp soda

Put in bowl in order listed. Mix baking powder, salt and soda gently into flour as you put in bowl. Mix all with beater until smooth. Bake on hot griddle.
Tip: Don't overcook! Bake each side only until "lightly" done and browned.

EASTER EGGS — Grandma Erb
(with note from Dad's wife, Mary)

Save all the brown and red skins from your onions way before Easter (just the dry parts.)

Put in a kettle with the raw eggs (as many as you need).

Boil until the eggs are done.

The more skins you have the darker the eggs and some will even have designs on them from the skins.

Note: I had to make these for your Dad every year as he thought they tasted better than ordinary boiled eggs. I still make them.

*****

Following are two recipes from Dad for making what we called Liverwurst when we were at home. Later Dad called it Liver Sausage. The second recipe was told to me by Dad when he was visiting once in the last few years. The first one was one that his wife, Mary, wrote down as he did it. It is probably the most accurate.

LIVER SAUSAGE   **Dad**
(with notes from Dad's wife, Mary)

About:
4 1/2 lbs pork jowls plus neck bones
6 lbs. pork shoulder with rind
2 lbs pork liver (beef won't work)
2 pork hocks or feet with skin

Cut up and cover with water and boil until done.
(The liver is put in last; about 45 min. or so.)

Run through a meat grinder.

Season with salt & pepper.

Mix all together and thin it with the water it was cooked in until it does not stick to your fingers.

Pack in cake pan and refrigerate over night (plastic works real good.) Cut into pieces, size for one meal and wrap and freeze.

Especially good with pancakes. You heat it up with lots of

raw onion and cook until the onions are done.

(Heart and tongue can be used if available.)

Note: I wrote it down one time as he was making it and then he looked it over and said it was as close as you could get as he did it from memory from helping his Dad make it. When his Dad made it he would cook the whole head of a hog and use all the meat from that.

We always had to have a sandwich made from the meat before it cooled.

LIVERWURST   **Dad**
(with note from Mom)

10 lbs pork roast, cut into 1 inch slices
6 to 8 clean hocks (with rind)
2 lbs good slab bacon
3 lbs liver

Cook in a big kettle until done. Add liver the last 45 minutes. Skim scum off. Take all bones out. Grind all meat together, save some juice. Put back in kettle. Add salt and pepper to taste. Cook, add some juice till sloppy. Smear in large cookies sheet or cake pan. Freeze. Cut.
To Cook: add onion, season while stir frying. *(This was usually served with pancakes.)*

Note: I always chopped the chunk of cold meat up and added just a little water to it, when heating it, to make it mushy enough to stir and cook the onion....Mom

MOM'S PANCAKES WITH MAPLE SYRUP

Mix pancakes according to Aunt Jemima box directions. Add vanilla to batter.

Mapleine Syrup: (from the back of the Mapleine box)

Instant Syrup:
Pour one cup boiling water over 2 cups sugar. Add ½ tsp Mapleine and stir. Makes 2 ¼ cups.

Thick Syrup:
2 Tbsp water
¼ cup sugar
1 ½ cups corn syrup
½ tsp Mapleine
Boil 2 minutes. Thickens as it cools. Makes 1 pint

OATMEAL PANCAKES   Diane

Mix: 1 ½ cup oatmeal
        2 cups buttermilk
Beat in: ½ cup flour
        1 tsp sugar
        1 tsp soda
        1 tsp salt
        2 beaten eggs

OMELETTES   Dad

Mix 2-3 eggs in small bowl until well combined. Place shortening in pan and heat to melt. Pour in eggs. Cook, lifting edges to let uncooked egg run into pan. When nearly set, flip with spatula. Salt and pepper. Flip back over and place desired ingredients on half of omelette. Fold over to cover. Remove from heat and serve.

OVEN BREAKFAST   Kim

2 cups (or more) shredded Cheddar or American cheese
2 lbs. sausage, browned and drained
12 eggs
1 cup cream

Butter a 9x13 inch pan. Place a thin layer of cheese on bottom. Break eggs on top; break yolks, but do not stir. Layer sausage on top of eggs. Put remaining cheese on top of sausage. Pour cream over all. (May use more cream if desired.) Cover; refrigerate overnight (a MUST). Bake uncovered at 350 degrees for one hour, or until top is browned and edges are bubbly. Let stand 5 minutes before cutting.

My First Cooking Experience

     Theresa sat in the cool shadows on the patio steps. Her bare toes curled around the top step. She hummed a little song to herself as she watched her toes. The little song went like this:
"Nobody likes me,
everybody hates me,
think I'll eat some worms.
Fat ones, skinny ones,
long ones, short ones,
any kind of worms at all.
Well, nobody likes me, everybody hates me..."
and so on, over and over. Theresa was having a little pity party for herself. That sunny summer morning her older sisters, Sheila and Rozanne, had decided to play together and they didn't want her tagging along. While she was finishing up her morning chores, they had disappeared and she couldn't find them anywhere when she went looking. So here she sat, singing and feeling pretty blue.

     She could hear her Mom in the kitchen through the front screen door. Soon steps came over and Mom said, "Nobody to play with you today?'

     Theresa shook her head, her ponytail bouncing.

     "Well," said Mom, "I need to make some Rice Krispy bars and I was wondering if maybe you could help me."

     Theresa jumped up, sisters forgotten, ready for something new. Mom didn't let the kids in the kitchen much, except for dishes and meals. Diane cooked once and awhile, but not the others. Occasionally Mom would offer to let Theresa help stir in chocolate chips when she made cookies or lick the beaters when she made a cake, but Theresa had never actually helped like a big person would. Like Diane, maybe.

Mom opened the door and patted Theresa on the head as she went by. Mom always seemed to know when Theresa needed a little extra attention. It wasn't easy being the youngest. Mom knew that, cause she was the youngest once herself.

Mom pretty much let Theresa make the Rice Krispy bars herself, with only words of guidance when it came to reading the recipe and heating the marshmallows and butter. Theresa stood by the stove on a chair; Mom right beside her, as she stirred the gooey mixture over a low heat. It was real important to have the heat low, Mom said, so the marshmallows wouldn't burn. Then Theresa mixed in the Rice Krispies and patted the mixture into the pan that Mom had prepared. Theresa felt such a sense of accomplishment when the bars were done. She was a cook! Just let those old sisters play alone. She had more important things to do. Maybe someday she might even be a professional cook!

Rice Krispy Bars
1/2 cup butter or margarine
40 large marshmallows
6 cups Rice Krispies
Heat butter and marshmallows together until melted. Stir in Rice Krispies and mix well. Pour into a greased 9x13 inch pan. Cool. Store tightly covered.

CAKES & FROSTINGS

APPLE CHUNK CAKE   Aunt Anna

1 cup sugar
1/2 cup oil or soft butter or margarine
2 eggs
2 tsp vanilla
2 cups flour
2 tsp soda
2 tsp cinnamon
½ tsp salt

Cream the first four ingredients. Make a well in center and add other ingredients and stir well. Add:
1 can apple pie filling
1 cup softened raisins
½ cup chopped nuts
Mix together. Pour in 9x13 greased pan. Sprinkle top with cinnamon and sugar mixture. Bake 350 degrees for 55 minutes or until done.
(Mom often put penuche frosting on this instead of cinnamon/sugar.)

APPLESAUCE CAKE   Grandma Erb

1 cup sugar plus a little brown sugar
2 eggs, beat well
1 cup sour cream with 1 tsp soda
1 tsp cinnamon
1 tsp vanilla
Dash of salt
2/3 cup applesauce
Flour as needed

APPLESAUCE CAKE   Vernice Erb

1 cup butter
2 cups sugar
2 eggs
1 tsp vanilla
3½ cup flour
3 ½ tsp soda
1 tsp cinnamon
1 tsp cloves
½ tsp nutmeg
1 tsp salt
3 small Tbsp cocoa
2 cups hot applesauce
1 cup raisins or chopped dates
1 cup chopped nuts

Bake slowly for 1 hour.

APPLESAUCE CAKE   Mom
(Sheila took this for a school project.)

3 cups flour, sifted before measuring
2 tsp soda
1 tsp each cinnamon, allspice, cloves
½ tsp nutmeg
½ tsp salt
1 cup sugar
1 cup raisins
1 cup nuts
½ cup butter, melted and cooled
2 cups applesauce

Sift together dry ingredients. Stir in raisins and nuts. Add butter and applesauce and mix well. Bake at 325 degrees for 1 hour or until done in a 9x13 pan..

BANANA CAKE   **Kim**

2-1/3 cups flour
1-2/3 cups sugar
1-1/4 cups mashed bananas (or more for heavier moister cake)
2/3 cup shortening
2/3 cup buttermilk
3 eggs
1-1/4 tsp baking powder
1-1/4 tsp baking soda
1 tsp salt

Bake 45-50 mins in a greased & floured 9x13" pan at 350 degrees. Frost with Banana Cake Frosting.

BANANA NUT CAKE   **Mom**

1 ½ cups brown sugar
2/3 cup shortening
2 eggs
1 tsp vanilla
2 cups flour
½ tsp soda
½ tsp salt
¼ cup buttermilk or sour milk
¾ cup coarsely chopped nuts
1 cup mashed bananas

Bake 350 degrees about 20 minutes.

BIRTHDAY CAKE WITH FROSTING   Mom

Mix and bake angel food cake according to box directions. Cool as directed and remove from pan. Place on large cake plate. Frost with Double Boiler Frosting.

Mom always cut a circle from cardboard and placed over the hole of the cake so the top would be smooth when she frosted it. She decorated it with packaged candy cake decorations and often sprinkled little colored dots on top.

Paul

CHOCOLATE CAKE — Grandma Erb

½ cup Crisco
1 cup sugar
Salt
1/3 cup cocoa with 1/3 cup cold water
2 ¼ cups sifted cake flour
1 cup cold water
1 tsp vanilla
3 egg whites, beaten
¾ cup sugar
1 ¼ tsp soda with 1 Tbsp boiling water

Cream Crisco and sugar. Blend in salt and cocoa with cold water. Add flour alternately with cold water. Add 1 tsp vanilla. Beat egg whites and add ¾ cup sugar to them. Fold into chocolate mixture. Last add soda and hot water.

COLD WATER DEVIL'S FOOD CAKE — Mom

1 ¼ cup sugar
½ cup shortening
2 sq melted chocolate*
2 unbeaten eggs
2 cups flour
1 tsp soda
½ tsp baking powder
¼ tsp salt
1 cup cold water
1 tsp vanilla

Mix all. Bake at 325 degrees in greased 9x13 pan until done.

*Mom used cocoa instead of chocolate. 3 Tbsp cocoa & 2 Tab shortening for each square.

EASY CHOCOLATE CAKE   Kim

1-1/2 cups flour
1 cup sugar
1 tsp baking soda
1 tsp salt
3 Tbsp cocoa
1 tsp vanilla
1 Tbsp vinegar
5 Tbsp oil
1 cup water

Mix all until smooth, bake in lightly-greased 8" cake pan, 350 degrees, 30
minutes or till done.

FRUIT CAKE   Velma Hoffman

½ cup lard
1 cup sugar
1 ½ cup applesauce
1 egg
1 cup raisins
1 cup dates
2 cups flour
1 tsp soda
1 tsp baking powder
½ tsp cinnamon
½ tsp nutmeg
¼ tsp cloves
vanilla
1 package fruit cake mix and nuts
275 degrees

FRUIT CAKE — **Aunt Vernie**

2 cups flour
1 cup sugar
pinch of salt
2 tsp soda
1 tsp cinnamon
1 tsp cloves
½ tsp nutmeg
3 Tbsp cocoa
1 Tbsp cornstarch

Sift and add:
1 cup nuts
1 cup raisins
Then add:
½ cup melted butter
1 ½ cup applesauce

Bake ½ to ¾ hour in slow oven. (Until barely done.) Frost with powdered sugar icing. Decorate with red cinnamon candies and sprinkles. Store in cool place to "ripen"-for at least one week.

GERMAN SWEET CHOCOLATE CAKE — **Mom**

1 package (4 oz) Baker's German Sweet Chocolate
½ cup water
2 cups flour
1 tsp baking soda
¼ tsp salt
1 cup softened butter or margarine
2 cups sugar
4 egg yolks
1 tsp vanilla
1 cup buttermilk
4 egg whites

Heat oven to 350 degrees. Line bottoms of three 9" cake pans with wax paper. Microwave chocolate and water in large microwavable bowl on HIGH 1 ½ to 2 minutes or until chocolate is almost melted, stirring halfway through the heating time. Stir until chocolate is completely melted. Mix flour, baking soda and salt; set aside. Beat butter and sugar in large bowl with electric mixer on medium speed until light and fluffy. Add egg yolks, 1 at a time, beating well after each addition. Stir in chocolate mixture and vanilla. Add flour mixture alternately with buttermilk, beating after each addition until smooth. Beat egg whites in another large bowl with electric mixer on high speed until stiff peaks form. Gently stir into batter. Pour into prepared pans. Bake 30 minutes or until cake springs back when lightly touched in center. Immediately run spatula between cakes and sides of pans. Cool 15 minutes; remove from pans. Remove wax paper. Cool completely on wire racks. Spread Coconut-Pecan Frosting between layers and over top of cake. Makes 12 servings.

Back: Theresa, Paul, Diane
Front: Kim, Rozanne, Sheila

HOT MILK CAKE **Diane**

4 eggs
2 cups sugar
2 cups flour
2 tsp baking powder
1 ½ tsp vanilla
1 cup milk
2 tsp butter

Beat eggs until thick and lemony. Gradually add sugar and beat well. Add flour, baking powder and vanilla. Heat milk and butter and beat into batter. Pour in greased 9x13 pan. Bake at 350 degrees 25-30 minutes or until done.

Dad & Mom (in the kitchen on the farm)

OATMEAL CAKE   Aunt Mabel

1½ cup boiling water
1 cup quick oats
½ cup dates, cut up
½ cup shortening
1 cup brown sugar
1 cup white sugar
2 eggs
1 tsp vanilla
1½ cup flour
½ tsp salt
1 tsp soda
½ cup chopped nuts

Place dates, oatmeal, and water in bowl. Let stand 20 minutes. Cream shortening and sugars; add eggs and vanilla. Beat well. Add dry ingredients and oatmeal mixture. Mix well. Bake at 375 degrees in a greased 9x13 pan for 30 minutes or until done. Frost with penuche frosting.

PEANUT CAKE   Great Aunt Lizzie
(This was Grace Erb's aunt)

2/3 cup butter
1 cup sugar
1 egg
1 cup sour milk
1¾ cup flour
1 tsp soda
1 tsp vanilla
1 cup ground salted peanuts (red skins on)

400 degrees for 10 minutes, then 350 degrees about 25 or 30 minutes.

PRUNE CAKE   **Great Aunt Barb**
(This was Grace Erb's aunt)

½ cup shortening
1 cup sugar
3 large eggs, beaten
½ cup buttermilk
2 cups flour
½ tsp salt
1 tsp baking powder
1 tsp cinnamon
1 tsp nutmeg
Nuts, optional
1 cup prunes

350 degrees in layer pans. Frost with penuche icing.

SOUR CREAM BURNT SUGAR CAKE
Jesse Young's Radio Show

Whip 1 cup sugar and 1 cup sour cream together. Add:
3 Tbsp burnt sugar syrup
¾ cup sweet milk
2 cups flour
¼ tsp cream of tartar
1 tsp baking powder
1 tsp soda
pinch of salt

Frost with Burnt Sugar Icing.

Jesse Young had a weekly radio cooking program that Anna Oswald and daughter, Grace (Erb) Oswald, would listen to when Grace was a child.

WACKY CAKE   Mom

Sift into an ungreased square cake pan:
1½ cups flour
1 cup sugar
1 tsp baking soda
1 tsp salt
3 Tbsp cocoa

Mix well. Make 3 holes. Into one pour 1 tsp vanilla, another put one Tbsp vinegar and the last put 5 Tbsp oil. Over all pour 1 cup boiling water. Mix well in pan. Bake 30 minutes. Cool. Good served with whipped cream. Cut and serve from pan.

WHITE CAKE   Grandma Erb

1½ cup sugar
½ cup butter
1 cup milk
2 cups flour for layer or 2 ½ cups for loaf
2 tsp baking powder
4 egg whites, beaten stiff
1 tsp vanilla

FROSTINGS:

BANANA CAKE FROSTING   Kim

1/3-2/3 cup shortening
6 Tbsp water (or more if needed)
dash salt
2 tsp vanilla
1/4 cup melted butter
powdered sugar (I usually use one whole bag)

Beat all together until smooth; spread on cooled cake.

COCONUT-PECAN FILLING AND FROSTING-Mom

1 can (12 oz) evaporated milk
1½ cups sugar
¾ cup butter or margarine
4 egg yolks, slightly beaten
1½ tsp vanilla
1 package (7 oz) Baker's Angel Flake coconut (about 2 2/3 cups)
1½ cups chopped pecans

Mix milk, sugar, butter, egg yolks and vanilla in large saucepan. Cook and stir on medium heat about 12 minutes or until thickened and golden brown. Remove from heat. Stir in coconut and pecans. Beat until cool and of spreading consistency. Makes about 4 ¼ cups.

DOUBLE-BOILER FROSTING   Mom
(*Sometimes called "7 minute icing"*)

1 egg white
¾ cup sugar
1/8 tsp cream of tartar
3 Tbsp water
½ tsp vanilla

Combine ingredients (except vanilla) in top of double-boiler, and beat to completely blend. Place over boiling water, and beat with rotary beater until mixture is fluffy and will hold its shape…5-7 minutes. Remove and blend in flavoring.

EASY PENUCHE FROSTING Mom

½ cup butter
1 cup packed brown sugar
¼ cup milk
1¾ to 2 cups sifted powdered sugar
Melt butter in saucepan. Stir in brown sugar. Boil and stir over low heat 2 minutes. Stir in milk. Bring to a boil, stirring constantly. Cool to lukewarm (120 degrees). Gradually add powdered sugar. Place pan in ice water and stir until thick enough to spread.

LUCILLE'S FROSTING
(Lucille Parks is a good friend of Mom's)

Beat until fluffy:
½ cup shortening
½ cup butter or margarine
1 cup sugar
1 egg
Beat in ½ cup warm milk 2 Tbsp at a time.
Beat until very fluffy. Add 1 tsp vanilla and beat well.

SOUR CREAM BURNT SUGAR CAKE FROSTING
Jesse Young's Radio Show

1 cup brown sugar
4 Tbsp cold water
1 egg white
Mix in double boiler. Beat over hot water until stiff peaks form. Then add some vanilla.
Jesse Young had a weekly radio cooking program that Anna Oswald and daughter, Grace (Erb) Oswald, would listen to when Grace was child.

Paul Cooks

Mom loved to cook so she encouraged each one of her kids to try their hand at it. Today it was Paul's turn in the kitchen. Theresa wondered what Paul would cook. Sheila had told her about Paul's cooking when they lived on the farm. But that was pretend, with dirt and grass. Surely he wouldn't cook like that now.

The other kids weren't allowed in the kitchen unless it was their turn to cook, and being a wintery Saturday morning, (with chores already done), it meant some time for cartoons. The girls lounged in the livingroom in front of the TV.

"Mom, I found a couple of recipes," Paul called. Mom left her bedroom where she was busy in the closet and went to the kitchen. After a bit of consulting, Paul was back at it and Mom passed through the livingroom on her way to the bedroom.

"What's he making, Mom?" Theresa wanted to know. She was curious about anything to do with cooking.

"Well," Mom said, "he found a recipe for Snickerdoodles and another for Potato Candy that he wants to try."

"What's a snickerdoodle?"

"Snickerdoodles are a cookie. Sort of like sugar cookies but with cinnamon."

"Oh," Theresa said. "Well, what kind of candy has potatoes in it?"

Mom chuckled. "I guess we'll find out soon enough." She went back to work.

Theresa watched the next episode of cartoons and was soon tired of The Flintstones. She really wanted to see what Paul was doing. A trip to the bathroom went through the kitchen. Maybe she could see something of interest.

She'd been lying on the couch. Getting up, she said, to no one in particular, "I'm going to the bathroom," and slowly headed to the kitchen.

Once around the corner, she paused, slightly hidden by the frig, and peeked into the kitchen. What a mess! On the stove boiled a pot of potatoes, in the sink were peelings (and a few peelings on the floor and on the counter.) Paul was standing with his back to her, mixing something in a big bowl at the far counter. He had flour and sugar canisters out and boxes and cans. There was a white patch on the floor where the flour had spilt. Theresa had seen enough. She went on to the bathroom and closed the door quietly behind her.

Boy! Was she glad she didn't have to clean up after Paul's cooking. He was barely into it and such a mess! Then an awful thought came to her. Maybe the girls would be expected to clean up after him! Paul didn't have to help in the kitchen too much anymore. When they'd been on the farm he had been Dad's helper and since they'd moved back to town, he hadn't been expected to help out in the house much. He often went to work as a hired hand for an older lady with her tree farm, and sometimes he went out to the Murphy's and helped on their dairy farm.

Theresa decided to go back to the TV and wait to see what would happen.

*****

Having tired of cartoons, the girls had scattered to different areas. Theresa had gone upstairs to finish her most recent mystery book featuring a young sleuth named Nancy Drew. She had read nearly all of the many books about Nancy. But she knew there were a few more on the shelf she hadn't read. After closing the book, she had thoughts about a jaunt to the Public Library to get some more books. It was only a few blocks away. She could smell cookies baking and thought maybe by now Paul would have samples.

In the kitchen things looked different. Cookies were stacked neatly on the table, some still cooling on the racks. The dishes were washed up and drying in the dish rack. Paul was at the counter, dipping round white balls into melted chocolate and placing them on a piece of wax paper. Chocolate drips were at a minimum.

No one else was around as Theresa stepped into the kitchen.

"How's it going?" she asked.

Paul looked up. "Pretty good. I'm almost done. Want to sample a cookie?"

Theresa nodded and plucked one off the rack. She bit into the sweet, flaky, cinnamony cookie. Delicious! She was quite impressed with her brother. All of that dirt cooking must have paid off in knowing how to cook. And she didn't have to help clean up! Now that was really sweet!

Note: I don't remember how the potato candy tasted, but I've included the recipe for you to try yourself!

Dad & Mom

CANDY

ALMOND BARK   Mom

Melt purchased almond bark according to directions. Add whole almonds. Spread on cookie sheet and cool. Break into pieces when set.
This was one of the candies Mom always made at Christmas when we were kids.

ALMOND BARK CANDY   Mom

½ large Almond Bark
Melt in 200 degree oven. Add:
¾ to 1 cup nuts
1 ¾ cup colored marshmallows
1 ½ to 2 cups Rice Krispies

BLACK WALNUT BRITTLE

2 cups sugar
1 cup white syrup
½ cup water
1 Tbsp butter
1½ cups walnuts
1 Tab soda
1 tsp vanilla

Cook sugar, syrup, and water until golden brown (300 degrees crack stage). Take off fire, add butter and nuts (or use 2 cups shelled roasted peanuts). Put on fire. Bring to a good bubble, remove and add soda. Stir and add vanilla. Pour on well buttered slab, then pull as it cools.

BEST-EVER POPCORN BALLS   Kimberly

8 Tbsp butter
1 cup sugar
1 cup brown sugar
1 cup white syrup
1 can sweetened condensed milk
2 tsp vanilla

Bring first 5 ingredients to a boil, add vanilla, boil 1 minute. Pour over 7-8 quarts popped corn, mix well, shape into balls.

CARAMELS   Aunt Verda

1 cup white sugar
½ cup butter or margarine
¾ cup dark syrup
1 cup light cream

Combine ingredients. Boil slowly till very hard ball stage. Add 1 tsp vanilla.

CARAMELS   Judy Oswald

1 cup sugar
¾ cup dark syrup
½ cup butter
1 cup light cream
½ cup walnuts
½ tsp vanilla

Combine sugar, syrup, butter, and ½ cup cream. Bring to a boil, stirring constantly. Add remaining ½ cream and cook slowly to very hard ball stage. Remove from heat. Add nuts and vanilla . Pour into creased 8" square pan. Mark in squares when pretty cool. Cut when cold. Wrap in wax paper.

CARAMELS   Theresa

2 lbs. brown sugar
2 cups butter
2 cups light corn syrup
1 can sweetened condensed milk

Bring to a boil. Boil to 245 to 250 degrees for the right firmness, depending on how soft you like them. Pour on a large buttered cookie sheet. Cool; cut and wrap.

CHRISTMAS BUTTERCRUNCH   Mom

1 cup butter cold from fridge (no substitutions)
1 cup sugar
1 ½ cup chopped walnuts
3 Tbsp cold water
1 Tbsp light corn syrup
1 cup milk chocolate chips

Use a heavy pan.
Say a prayer that this turns out right.
Lightly butter cookie sheet
Chop nuts; separate 1 cup and ½ cup
Mix water and syrup together in cup
Chunk butter and melt over low-med heat
Add 1 cup sugar, a little at a time, stirring constantly. Cook and stir over med to med low heat until all one consistency. It takes a little while.
Remove from heat and add syrup/water mixture. Mix well and return to heat.

Cook over med to med low heat, stirring occasionally, until it begins to brown on edges. This takes a little while. Watch closely. Clean sides of pan with spatula when necessary.

Add candy thermometer and continue to cook until 290 degrees stirring occasionally. Clean sides as necessary.

At 290 degrees, remover thermometer, add 1 cup nuts and cook and stir 3 minutes.

Pour into prepared pan. Spread to thick/thinness desired.

Sprinkle chips over evenly. Cover with another cookie sheet. Let set a few minutes until chips melt.

Uncover; spread chips to cover.

Sprinkle remaining ½ cup nuts evenly over. Press into chips with the bake of a spatula.

Cool in fridge.

Break into pieces.

Store in frig or freezer.

Enjoy and be thankful this turned out!

When we were kids, Mom would sometimes put chocolate and nuts on both sides.

CORN FLAKE CANDY   Velma Hoffman

1 cup sugar
1 cup white corn syrup
1 cup cream
Boil to soft ball stage (240 degrees). Add:
1 tsp vanilla
6 cups corn flakes
1 cup salted peanuts (or other)
1 cup chopped walnuts.
Mix altogether. Pat loosely in 9x13 pan. Cool. Cut in squares.

DIVINITY   **Velma Hoffman**

2 cups sugar
½ cup water
½ cup syrup
Boil all together until crisp when a little is dropped in cold water. Then pour slowly over the beaten whites of two eggs, beating as you pour. When white add 1 cup walnuts and a little flavoring.

NEVER FAIL FUDGE   **Mom**

1/3 cup butter
4 ½ cups sugar
1 can (14 ½ oz) can evaporated milk
1 cup marshmallow crème
1 bar (13 oz) Hershey's sweet chocolate, grated
2 pkgs (12 oz) semi sweet chocolate chips
2 Tbsp vanilla
2 cups chopped nuts

Combine butter, sugar, and milk. Boil 5½ minutes. Remove from heat and add remaining ingredients except nuts. Beat until well mixed. Add nuts. Spoon into buttered pan. Cool until firm, then cut. Makes 5 lbs.

Note on bottom of card from Mom:
"Stir constantly while cooking. I like to use 1 – 12 oz package of milk chocolate chips in place of the grated bar. May also substitute 12 cut marshmallows for marshmallow crème."

MAPLE FUDGE   Grandma Erb

3 cups brown sugar
1 cup cream
1 tsp maple flavoring
1 cup nuts

Boil sugar and cream to soft ball stage. Beat until light. Add nuts and flavoring. Turn into buttered dish.

PEANUT BRITTLE   Rozanne

1 ½ cup sugar
1 cup light corn syrup
1 cup water
12-16 oz raw Spanish peanuts
2 Tbsp butter
1 tsp soda
1 tsp water
1 ½ tsp vanilla

Boil sugar, water and corn syrup in dutch oven to 234 degrees over medium to medium high heat. Remove from heat and add peanuts and butter. Turn to medium heat and cook to exactly 300 degrees, stirring constantly. Add vanilla, water and soda, previously mixed together. Stir and put on buttered cookie sheet. Spread to thick/thinness desired. When cool, break in pieces and store in plastic bag or container. Never put in refrigerator.

POPCORN BALLS

1 cup light syrup
½ cup sugar
1 tsp cream of tartar
Boil to hard ball stage. Add:
1 tsp butter
¼ tsp soda
Pour over 4 qts popcorn. Cool slightly and shape into balls.

POTATO CANDY   Paul

¼ cup mashed potatoes
1 tsp vanilla
1 tsp butter
1 ½ cup powdered sugar
1 ½ cup coconut

Mix and chill. Form into balls and chill again.
Melt:
4 squares semi sweet chocolate
1 piece wax paraffin the size of 1 square of chocolate
Dip balls in chocolate and place on wax paper.

TAFFY   Diane

2 cups brown sugar
¼ cup dark syrup
2 Tbsp vinegar
2 Tbsp water
1 tsp salt
¼ cup butter
2 tsp vanilla

Cook together sugar, syrup, vinegar, water and salt. Boil until it becomes brittle in water. When almost done, add butter. Add vanilla just before turning into buttered pan. Cool and pull.

SWEETENED CONDENSED MILK   Kim
(handy at Christmas time!)

1 cup powdered sugar
2/3 cup sugar
1/3 cup boiling water
3 Tbsp melted butter

Combine all in blender; blend 1 minute. Makes 14 oz.

Grandma, Aunt Ellen & Grandpa in the Cafe

CANNING & PRESERVING

JAMS & JELLIES:

BEET JELLY   Mom

6 cups beet juice
½ cup lemon juice
2 boxes Sure-Jell
8 cups sugar
1 box raspberry gelatin

Bring beet juice, lemon juice and Sure-Jell to a boil. Add sugar and raspberry gelatin and boil for 6 minutes. A variation of the recipe is to use wild or tame grape juice instead of beet juice and omit lemon juice. Use lime gelatin instead of raspberry with this variation. Seal the jelly with paraffin and store like any jelly.

CRABAPPLE BUTTER

Wash and cut lengthwise in half. Cut out blossom and stem ends. To boil apples, put ½ " water above crabapples. Boil 45 minutes. Then put thru food mill (use juice too). To 10 cups pulp, add 5 cups sugar, grated rind of 1 lemon, and juice of 1 lemon. Add 1 Tbsp cinnamon, heaped a little, and ½ Tbsp cloves. Cook until thick and clear, about 45 minutes to an hour or so.
For 12 cups pulp use:
6 cups sugar
1 lemon, juice and rind
A little more cinnamon and cloves
Cook 45 minutes or so. Makes 6 ½ pints.

This recipe is from Dollie Hanson's (our neighbor) Aunt Martha.

RHUBARB JAM — Grandma Erb

6 cups rhubarb, cut up
4 cups sugar, stand over night
1 can apricot pie filling
1 orange gelatin
1/3 cup orange peel, if desired

Boil rhubarb, sugar and pie filling for 10 minutes; add gelatin and orange peel..

Note on bottom of card: Mom Erb says she used the grated peel of 1 orange.

RHUBARB JELLY — Aunt Verda

5 cups rhubarb, cut fine
3 cups sugar
1 box red jello (any flavor)

Let the rhubarb and sugar stand till juicy. Boil 15 minutes. Add jello. Boil 1 minute and put in jars and seal.

STRAWBERRY JAM — Grandma Erb

Quart of strawberries in colander. Two qts boiling water through them. Drain. Put off stems. Add 2 cups sugar. Shake. Let stand till juice forms. Put on stove, bring to boil. Boil 2 minutes. Slowly add two cups sugar. Boil 5 minutes more. Stand 24 hours then seal with wax.

This was in Grandma's handwriting on the back of an envelope postmarked 1948. I printed it exactly as she had written it, even though the directions seemed odd to me.

TRIPLE BERRY JAM   Theresa

4 cups fresh or frozen blueberries
2 ½ cups fresh or frozen red raspberries
2 ½ cups fresh or frozen strawberries
¼ cup lemon juice
2 pkgs (1 ¾ oz each) powdered fruit pectin
11 cups sugar

Combine the berries and lemon juice in large kettle; crush fruit slightly. Stir in pectin. Bring to a full rolling boil over high heat, stirring constantly. Stir in sugar, return to a full rolling boil. Boil 1 minute, stirring constantly. Remove from the heat, skim off any foam. Pour hot into hot jars, leaving ¼ inch head space. Adjust caps. Process for 15 minutes in a boiling water bath. Yield: about six pints.

PICKLES & RELISHES:

BREAD AND BUTTER PICKLES   Grandma Erb

5 medium cucumbers
3 medium onions
¼ cup salt
1 cup vinegar
½ tsp celery salt
1 cup water
½ tsp mustard seed
¾ cup sugar
½ tsp ginger
¼ cups turmeric

Wash cucumbers. Cut in thin slices. Peel and slice onions. Combine. Add salt. Let stand 2 hours. Drain. Heat remaining ingredients to boiling. Add cucumbers and onions. Boil slowly until tender. Pack while hot in jars.

CHUNK PICKLES   Grandma Erb

Medium sized pickles, cut in chunks or thick slices. Put in salt brine. Let stand 3 days. Drain. Put in clear water 3 days. (Change water each of the 3 days.) 7th day-to 1 cup sugar, 6 cups water, add alum the size of a walnut. Simmer pickles for 2 hours. (Do not boil.) Drain. (Throw juice away.) To 5 cups sugar, 2 cups vinegar, 1 cup water, 1 oz stick cinnamon, 1 oz. whole allspice, add pickles and cook to boiling point.

CRISP SWEET PICKLES   Grandma Erb

Use any size cukes. Wash and put in jars. Pour boiling water over. Let stand overnight. Drain, cover again with boiling water. Repeat for 5 successive mornings; 6 in all. On the 7th morning add enough salt so water does not taste flat. On 8th morning pack in jars. If large cucumbers are

used, cut into one inch chunks. Cover with the following syrup:
1 cup vinegar
¼ tsp turmeric
1 tsp celery seed
2 cups sugar
1 Tbsp mixed pickling spices.
Seal while hot.

CRISPY SWEET PICKLES   Ruth Ann

1 qt dark vinegar
1 ½ Tbsp pickling salt
2 Tbsp pickling spice
8 cups sugar (5-6 cups will do fine)

Fill gallon jar with washed, medium sized cucumbers. Boil water and fill jar to top, cover lightly. The next two days empty jar and refill with boiling water. On fourth day, empty jar and cut cucumbers into ½ inch chunks. Heat above ingredients. Pour into jar, the next two days reheat and put back into jar. On the fourth day heat again, put cucumbers into pints, fill up and seal. Always stays crispy.

HAMBURGER DILLS   Aunt Verda

BRINE:
¼ cup vinegar
1 ½ cup water
1 heaping tsp salt
2 cups sugar

Pack sliced cukes, one sprig dill and one large sliced onion. Bring to a boil in canner. Let cool in canner. Makes 2 qts.

NEVER FAIL DILL PICKLES   Ruth Ann

1 qt water
½ cup canning salt
½ qt dark vinegar
Wash tiny cucumbers, put into jars with 1 piece dill and 2 garlic buds, this is for pints. Boil water, vinegar and salt for several minutes. Pour into jars and seal.

SO SIMPLE SWEET PICKLES   Grandma Erb

Small cucumbers
3 qts vinegar
2 qts water
1 cup salt
1 Tbsp ground mustard
1 tsp saccharin
½ tsp powdered alum
2 oz pickling spices

Wash cucumbers and dry. Pack in jars (10-12 qts). Mix the other ingredients and pour over pickles (cold, do not heat), seal jars. Let stand several weeks before using.

Grandma wrote 'Henrietta' on the bottom of this recipe. I'm assuming it came from her long time friend, Henrietta Hauder.

SOCIETY CHIP PICKLES   Aunt Mabel

18 dill pickles
Wash and pack in crock and cover with boiling water. Cover with fresh boiling water for 3 days. On 4th morning, cut in about ¼ inch circular slices.
Heat:

1 qt vinegar
8 cups sugar
1 ½ Tbsp pickling salt
2 Tbsp pickling spice
Pour over drained pickles in jars. Reheat for 2 mornings. On the 4th morning, reheat, pour over pickles and seal.

SPICED BEETS   Grandma Erb

2 cups sugar
2 cups syrup or honey
1 qt vinegar
1 qt water
1 Tbsp cinnamon
2 tsp allspice
1 Tbsp horseradish

Cook beets in salt water, peel, pack in jars, fill with pickling syrup made of above ingredients, and boil 5 minutes.

BEET RELISH   Grandma Erb

1 qt each beets and cabbage
½ cup horseradish
2 cups vinegar
1 ½ cups sugar
1 tsp salt
1 tsp mustard seed

Boil beets, slip skins off, chop. Chop cabbage. Boil vinegar, salt, sugar, mustard seeds. Pour over above mixture. Seal while hot.

CORN RELISH — Grandma Erb

Cut corn from 18 ears corn. Chop head cabbage, 4 green peppers, 4 large onions, 1 can pimentos. Combine with the following:
1 ½ qts vinegar, 3 cups sugar, 1 Tbsp mustard seed & ½ cup salt
Boil 20 minutes. Seal while hot.

CUCUMBER CARROT RELISH — Ruth Ann

7 cups ground cucumbers
4 large peppers, ground
3 large onions, ground
5 cups ground carrots

Sprinkle 1 Tbsp canning salt over and let set 2-3 hours. Drain well. Add:
1 Tbsp mustard seeds
1 Tbsp celery seeds
5 cups sugar
3 cups dark vinegar

Boil 2 minutes and seal in pints while hot. Mix with miracle whip. Makes an excellent dip for all seafood.

MISC:

APPLESAUCE — Theresa

Put 1 qt. water and 1 tsp salt in large Dutch oven. Fill with pared, quartered apples. Drain off ½ liquid. Cook till mushy; add approximately 1 ½ cup sugar (or to taste). Put in jars. Process 20 minutes in boiling water bath.

BAKED CREAMED FREEZER CORN — Theresa

Fill roaster pan nearly full (about 1-2 inches from top) with corn cut raw from cob. (Approximately 3 dozen large ears.) Add 1 pint cream and 1 lb. real butter, cut up. Bake 1 to 1 ¼ hours at 350 degrees, stirring about every 15 minutes. Cool pan in sink full of water. Package and freeze. Makes about 1 dozen pint and a half bags.

FRUIT SYRUP FOR PANCAKES — Mom

4 cups juice
2 cups sugar
1 cup white syrup
Boil 3 minutes. Pour into hot jars and seal. 4 pints. Refrigerate after opening.

Note: For Chokecherry, use 3 cups chokecherry juice and 1 cup apple juice.

HOMEMADE TOMATO SOUP — Aunt Verda

Sauté 6 chopped onions, 1 bunch celery, chopped and add 8 qts tomatoes quartered. Cook all until tender, and then run all through a sieve. To pulp add 1 cup sugar, 1 cup flour, ¼ cup salt, 1 cup butter. Cook until desired thickness, seal boiling hot in jars.

PICKLED FISH — Gene Jindra
(Gene was a cop with Dad.)

48 hrs - pickling salt & water
48 hrs - white vinegar
48 hours in brine:
4 cups white vinegar
3 cups sugar

1 cup white wine
Pickling spice and onion
Bay leaf

V-8 TOMATO JUICE   **Aunt Verda**

8 lbs. tomatoes
½ cup chopped onion
1 cup chopped celery
2 tsp Worcestershire sauce
½ cup lemon juice
2 tsp salt
1 Tbsp sugar
¼ tsp hot sauce

Cook tomatoes, onion, and celery for 15 minutes. Strain; add rest of the ingredients and bring to a boil. Add some water.

Aunt Anna, Cousin Ruth Ann, Aunt Mabel, Grandma

Erb Family Cookbook
Bonanza

One of the few TV shows Mom allowed the children to watch was the popular western called "Bonanza". Bonanza was the story of a rancher in Utah named Ben Cartwright. Ben and his three grown sons, Adam, Hoss and Little Joe, lived on the Ponderosa. There was no Mrs. Cartwright, only a little Chinese man named Hop-Sing, who did all the things a Mrs. Cartwright should have done, so there really wasn't a need for her and no one ever questioned that.

Every Saturday night the family gathered in the big living room at the other end of the big dining room and would tune in the black and white TV. Rozanne, Sheila, and Theresa would line up on the floor in front of the TV, sitting cross-legged and absorbing all that happened to those cowboys and their ranch. In their excitement they would inch closer to the TV and mom would repeatedly remind them to move back.

This program was the source of many hours of playing "cowboys". Old bikes were suddenly fabulous steeds, ready to carry them to the far corners of their own ranch. Three little girls were transformed into Adam, Hoss and Little Joe. There was often an argument over who would be Little Joe, as all three girls thought him the most handsome. Theresa always thought the privilege should belong to her as she was the youngest, same as Little Joe (called that because of his age, not size), but Rozanne and Sheila didn't see it that way at all.

After a hard day on the range, the three little hungry "cowboys" would raid the chuck house for food. Their favorite was "the hamburger". Mom was a wonderful baker. She made absolutely the best molasses cookies ever. They were big--almost as big across as a hungry child's stretched flat hand. And perfectly, evenly flat. Sugar sparkled on them and they were best warm straight from the oven, because the edges were just slightly crispy, but the center was doughy soft. These cookies became the "hamburger" in a favorite snack for three little "cowboys".

Following is the recipe for the cookies, with directions on how to assemble the very popular "hamburger".

CHOCOLATE GINGERSNAPS

(For the popular "hamburger")
(Mom developed this recipe herself after eating lumberjack gingersnaps while visiting The Logging Camp in Park Rapids.)

1 cup sugar
¼ cup butter or margarine
½ cup shortening
1 egg
¼ cup molasses
1 ¾ cup flour
1 ½ tsp soda
4 Tbsp cocoa
1 tsp cinnamon
½ tsp each of cloves, nutmeg, ginger, allspice & salt

Form into balls. Roll in sugar. Place on ungreased sheets. Bake at 350 degrees for 12 minutes or until top cracks.

Two ways to bake – both good!

1. Flatten real thin with glass dipped in sugar, springle more sugar on top and bake-not too long-watch carefully!
2. Roll in balls the size of large walnuts, then roll in powdered sugar. Bake only until they are all cracked on tops, then take out. Don't bake too long; they will be soft inside and chewy. Good!

Hamburgers
2 slices of white bread
1 full sized Chocolate Gingersnap Cookie
Childlike Imagination
Place the cookie between the white bread and pretend!

Note: The best bread for this sandwich is the white, light, fluffy bread that local stores sell the cheapest.

Kimberly, Theresa, Dad, Rozanne, Paul, Diane, Mom, Sheila
(mid 1990's)

COOKIES

AMISH LEBKUCHEN — Mom

1 cup honey
1 cup dark syrup or molasses
½ cup brown sugar
2 eggs
2 heaping Tbsp vegetable shortening
6 cups flour
1 ½ Tbsp soda

With electric mixer, mix first 4 ingredients at least ten minutes. Add the rest of the ingredients, blending well. Form dough into 8" long rolls, wrap in wax paper and refrigerate overnight.

Cut into ¼" thick slices. On greased cookie sheets bake 325 degrees about 12 minutes. Cool and frost with vanilla icing and if you like, sprinkle with colored sugar.

APPLESAUCE COOKIES — Grandma Erb

1 cup shortening
2 cups sugar
2 cups applesauce
2 beaten eggs
4 cups flour
½ tsp salt
2 tsp soda
1 tsp cinnamon
Raisins and/or nuts

Mix shortening and sugar. Add eggs and applesauce.

Combine dry ingredients and add to other mixture. Add raisins and nuts. Bake on greased sheets at 375 degrees 10-12 minutes.

BANANA DROPS   Mom

1 cup butter
2 cups sugar
3 eggs, well beaten
1 tsp vanilla
4 cups flour
2 tsp baking powder
½ tsp soda
1 tsp salt
1 ½ cup mashed bananas
¼ cup nuts

Place half of walnut meat in the center of each cookie. Bake 400 degrees for 12 minutes.

BANANA OATMEAL COOKIES   Mom

1 ½ cup flour
1 tsp soda
½ tsp salt
¼ tsp nutmeg
¾ tsp cinnamon
¾ cup shortening
1 cup sugar
1 egg
1 cup mashed banana
1¾ cup oatmeal

400 degrees for 15 minutes. Drop cookies.

BOILED RAISIN COOKIES   Grandma Erb

2 cups raisins
¾ cup water
3 cups sugar
1 ½ cup shortening
3 eggs
6 cups flour
2 tsp soda in 1/3 cup hot water
1 tsp nutmeg
1 tsp cinnamon
Nuts, optional

Boil 2 cups of raisins with ¾ cup water until done. Drain and save juice. Cool raisins. Cream sugar and shortening. Add eggs and raisin juice. Combine dry ingredients and mix in. Add soda/water. Mix well. Add raisins and nuts. Drop by spoonfuls on greased pan. Bake at 350 degrees until done.

BROWN SUGAR COOKIES   Grandma Erb

1 ½ cups brown sugar
1 cup shortening, not quite full
2 eggs
1 ½ tsp vanilla
½ tsp salt
1 tsp soda in ¼ cup warm water
2 ½ cups flour, maybe a little more

Mix and bake at 350 degrees for 10-12 minutes. You may use nuts or raisins or both.

BUCK HILL COOKIES   Mom

1 cup oleo or butter
1 cup sugar
1 cup brown sugar
1 cup oil
2 tsp vanilla
3½ cup flour
1 tsp soda
1 tsp cream of tartar
½ cup oatmeal
½ cup coconut
6 oz chocolate or butterscotch chips
1 cup Rice Krispies

Bake 350 degrees 10-15 minutes.

Note: this does not have eggs. (Don't add any!) Also, Mom has used half butter and half Crisco for the oleo and it was good.

BUTTERSCOTCH COOKIES
Great Grandma Oswald

½ cup butter
½ cup lard or butter flavor Crisco (lard is best)
2 cups brown sugar
2 eggs
3 cups flour
1 tsp cream of tartar
1 tsp soda
2 ½ tsp vanilla

Mix in order given. Pack in loaf and chill. Slice and bake at 350 degrees.
Note: may add ½ cup chopped nuts.

CARAMEL CREAM SANDWICH COOKIES   Mom

1 cup butter or oleo
¾ cup brown sugar
1 unbeaten egg yolk
2 ¼ flour

Chill for easier handling. Shape into balls the size of a marble. Place on ungreased cookie sheets, flatten to 1/8" thick. Mark a design with a fork. Bake 325 degrees for 9-12 minutes. Remove from sheets. Cool. Put together with Burnt Sugar Frosting:
Brown 2 Tbsp butter in saucepan. Remove from heat. Blend in 1 ½ cup powdered sugar gradually. Add ½ tsp vanilla and 4-5 tsp cream until spreading consistency.

CHOCOLATE CHIP COOKIES   Mom

½ cup soft oleo
1/3 cup shortening
1 cup sugar
1 cup brown sugar
2 eggs
2 tsp vanilla
3 ½ cups sifted flour
1 tsp salt
1 tsp soda
12 oz chocolate chips

Bake on greased sheets 8 minutes at 375 degrees. Don't bake any longer than 10 minutes.

CHOCOLATE CHIP COOKIES   Theresa

1 cup butter flavored Crisco
1 cup brown sugar
3 large eggs
1 ½ tsp vanilla
1 small pkg instant vanilla pudding
2½ cup flour
1 tsp soda
1 - 12 oz chocolate chips
Bake at 375 degrees on greased sheets, 8-10 minutes.

CHOCOLATE DROP COOKIES   Mom

2 cups brown sugar
1 cup shortening
2 eggs
1 cup milk
2 tsp vanilla
½ tsp salt
3 cups flour
1 tsp soda
½ cup cocoa

Chill. Bake at 350 degrees.

Frosting:
3 cups powdered sugar
6 Tbsp cocoa
3 Tbsp melt oleo
½ tsp vanilla
Add enough hot water to make it easy to spread.

CHOCOLATE MARSHMALLOW KISSES
Aunt Lois

1¾ cup flour
½ cup cocoa
1 tsp soda
½ tsp salt
1 cup sugar
½ cup shortening
2 eggs
1 tsp vanilla
nuts and marshmallows

Mix. Resembles pie dough. Place a few pecans on greased cookie sheet. Roll dough in walnut sized balls and press lightly on each nut cluster. Bake 8 minutes at 350 degrees. Cut marshmallows in half and place half cut side down on each cookie. Return to oven and bake 2 minutes. When cookies are cool, frost.
Frosting:
6 oz chocolate chips
½ cup canned milk
¼ cup butter or oleo
Cook, stirring constantly till blended. Boil two minutes. Add powdered sugar until spreading consistency. Spread over cookies.

CHRISTMAS SUGAR SHAPES   **Mom**

1 cup oleo margarine
2 cups sugar
2 beaten eggs
2 tsp vanilla
½ cup milk
5 cups flour
1 tsp salt
1 tsp soda

Mix; chill; roll, and cut. Bake on greased sheets 8-10 minutes at 400 degrees or until lightly browned. Frost with a powdered sugar frosting.

DATE FILLED COOKIES   **Grandma Erb**

2 cups brown sugar
1 cup shortening
2 eggs
1 ½ tsp soda dissolved in ¼ cup warm water
1 tsp salt
1 tsp vanilla
3 ½ cups flour
1 cup quick oats
½ cup nuts

FILLING:
1 small pkg dates
1 cup sugar
2 Tbsp flour
1 cup cold water
a little butter or lemon juice

Cook and cool filling. Drop dough and make a nest in center. Put in some filling and them put a small bit of dough on top. Bake at 350-375 degrees.

DATE PINWHEELS   **Mom**

1 lb. pitted dates
½ cup water
½ cup sugar
1 cup finely chopped nuts
Cook dates, sugar and water until thick. Cool and add

chopped nuts.
½ cup butter
½ cup brown sugar
½ cup white sugar
1 beaten egg
2 cups flour
½ tsp soda
½ tsp salt
½ tsp vanilla

Mix well. Chill if necessary. Dough is thick, so may not need to chill. Roll out and spread date mixture on top. Roll up. Chill, slice and bake 350 degrees about 8 minutes. Watch closely because they can brown quickly.

Note: Mom says it works best if you freeze roll for easier slicing and rinse knife under hot water for each cutting; this prevents the filling from squashing.

DELICIOUS COOKIES   Rozanne

1 cup butter
1 cup oil
1 cup brown sugar
1 tsp butter flavor
1 tsp coconut flavor
1 tsp vanilla
1 tsp cream of tartar
1 tsp soda
1 cup each of oats, Rice Krispies, and coconut
12 oz butterscotch chips

Bake 350 degrees for appr. 12 minutes.

DOROTHY YODER'S COOKIES — Mom

(The Yoders were friends from the Mennonite Church in Minot, where we lived for a short time.)

2/3 cup butter
1½ cup brown sugar
2 eggs
1 tsp vanilla
1 Tbsp vinegar
1 cup evaporated milk
2 ½ cups flour
1 tsp soda
½ tsp baking powder
½ tsp salt
1 cup walnuts

Mix and bake at 350 degrees for 15 minutes. Frost with the following:
Icing:
½ cup butter
3 cups sifted powder sugar
¼ cup boiling water

Melt butter till light brown, add sugar, then water. Beat until it holds its shape.

EASY OATMEAL COOKIES — Grandma Erb

¾ cup sifted flour
½ tsp salt
½ tsp soda
½ cup shortening
½ cup brown sugar
½ cup white sugar
½ tsp vanilla
1 egg
1½ cup quick oatmeal

Bake at 350 degrees for 10-12 minutes.

FARM HOUSE COOKIES   **Mom**
(one of Diane's favorites)

1 cup shortening (butter, margarine or shortening)
2 cups sugar
2 eggs
1 cup sour cream
1 tsp vanilla
½ tsp soda
4 tsp baking powder
4 ½ cups flour
½ tsp salt
¾ cup nuts

Cream shortening and sugar together. Add eggs one at a time, continuing to beat. Add sour cream and vanilla. Sift dry ingredients and add to creamed mixture. Roll on floured canvas, fairly thick. Cut with large round cutter. Place on cookie sheet. Sprinkle with chopped nuts or decorate with raisins. Bake at 350 degrees for 15-18 minutes. These cookies should be large, soft and thick.

FRUIT COOKIES   **Great Grandma Oswald**

1 cup sugar
½ cup butter
2 eggs
½ cup milk
1 tsp vanilla
2 tsp baking powder
1 tsp cinnamon
2¼ cup flour
1 cup raisins
1 cup nuts

Cut up nuts and raisins. Mix all together. Roll out on floured board. Spread top with milk or cream; sprinkle with sugar. Cut with cutter. Place on greased cookie sheet. Bake 375 degrees for 10-12 minutes.

GINGIES   Diane

1/3 cup oleo
1 cup brown sugar
1½ cup molasses
2/3 cup cold water
6 cups flour
2 tsp soda
1 tsp salt
1 tsp each ginger, allspice, cloves, cinnamon

Mix and chill several hours or overnight. Roll out thick. Cut and place 1 inch apart on lightly greased sheets. Bake at 350 degrees for 15 minutes.

GINGER CREAMS   Grandma Erb

1 cup shortening
1 cup brown sugar
¾ cup unsulphered molasses
¾ cup hot water
2 eggs
½ tsp soda
4 cups flour
2 tsp cinnamon
½ tsp ginger
½ tsp salt

Drop on sheet. Bake at 350 degrees 12-15 minutes. Frost while warm with powdered sugar icing.

GINGER LACE COOKIES   Mom

1 cup sugar
¾ cup shortening
4 Tbsp molasses (orange label is best)
1 beaten egg
2 cups flour
2 tsp soda
1 tsp ginger
1 tsp cinnamon
pinch of salt

Shape into balls a little larger than walnuts, (depends on how big of cookies you like) roll in granulated sugar. Bake about 12 minutes at 375 degrees.

GRAHAM CRACKER COOKIES   Ruth Ann

Fill a large cookie sheet with graham crackers.
1 stick butter or margarine
1 cup brown sugar
1 cup chopped nuts (may use less)

Cook 2 minutes. Spread on crackers and bake 8 minutes at 350 degrees. Quick and easy and everyone seems to enjoy.

GUMDROP COOKIES   Sue Erb

1 ½ cup brown sugar
1 cup Crisco or shortening
2 eggs
1 tsp baking powder
1 tsp soda
½ cup coconut

1 cup oatmeal
2 cups flour
1 box orange slices (cut about size of marbles) OR gumdrops, but no black ones.

Mix all well. Bake at 350 degrees for 10-12 minutes.

HAWAIIAN DROP COOKIES   Grandma Erb

2/3 cup shortening
1 ¼ cup sugar
1 egg
½ tsp vanilla
½ tsp almond flavor
¾ cup crushed pineapple, drained
½ cup coconut
2 cups sifted flour
2 tsp baking powder
½ tsp salt

Mix as for drop cookies.

ICE BOX COOKIES   Grandma Erb

1 cup shortening
2 cups brown sugar
4 cups flour
1 cup chopped nuts
1 cup chopped dates
1 tsp salt
4 eggs
1 tsp each soda, baking powder, cinnamon, nutmeg & vanilla

Mix in order given, chill, slice & bake in 400 degree oven.

ICE BOX COOKIES   Mom

2 cups brown sugar
½ cup butter
½ cup lard   (Mom likes to use all butter.)
2 eggs
1 tsp vanilla
4 cups flour
1 tsp soda
1 tsp cream of tartar
pinch of salt
1 cup chopped nuts

Chill, slice and bake at 350 to 375 degrees.

MAPELINE CRUNCHIES   Mom
2 cups flour
3½ tsp baking powder
½ tsp salt
1 cup shortening
1 cup white sugar
1 cup brown sugar
2 eggs
2 tsp Mapeline
1 cup coconut
2 cups oatmeal
2 cups wheat or corn flakes

Mix all and drop on greased baking sheet at 375 degrees. 7 dozen cookies.

MILLION DOLLAR COOKIES   Mom

1 cup vegetable shortening
½ cup white sugar
½ cup brown sugar

1 egg
½ tsp almond flavoring
½ tsp vanilla
2 cups flour
1 tsp cream of tartar
1 tsp soda

Drop by teaspoons onto cookie sheets and press them with glass bottom which has been dipped in sugar. The thinner you make the cookies the better they are. (Do not use butter.)

MONSTER COOKIES   Mom

1 cup sugar
½ pound brown sugar (1 cup packed)
¾ pound peanut butter (1½ cup)
¼ pound butter (½ cup)
3 eggs
½ tsp vanilla
1 ½ tsp corn syrup
4 ½ cups oatmeal
2 tsp soda
½ pound M&Ms
4 oz chocolate chips
350 degrees 6-8 minutes. (May make any size you want.)

NO BAKE COOKIES   Mom

Combine in saucepan:
2 cups sugar
½ cup cocoa
½ cup milk
½ cup butter

Bring to a boil and boil 1 minute. Add:
½ cup peanut butter
1 tsp vanilla
Mix to melt P.B. then add:
3 cups uncooked, quick oatmeal
Mix well and drop by tsps onto waxed paper.

OATMEAL COOKIES   Grandma Erb

2 cups sifted flour
1 tsp soda
½ tsp salt
2 cups quick oatmeal
½ cup packed brown sugar
1 cup shortening
1/3 cup milk (sweet or soured)
2 beaten eggs
1 tsp vanilla

OATMEAL COOKIES   Aunt Mabel

¾ cup shortening
½ cup sugar, brown or white
½ cup syrup or molasses
2 beaten eggs
2 Tbsp milk
2 cups flour
2 cups oatmeal
1 tsp soda
1 tsp cinnamon
½ tsp nutmeg
pinch of salt
nuts and raisins

Mix all together and drop by tsps on greased baking sheet.

OLD FASHIONED SUGAR COOKIES
Grandma Erb

2 cups sugar
1 cup butter
3 eggs
1 cup soured cream (not commercial)
1 tsp soda
1 tsp vanilla
4 cups flour

Mix together sugar and butter. Add eggs and sour cream and vanilla. Add flour and soda. Mix well. May need a little more flour so the dough is easy to handle. Roll out, cut, and bake on buttered cookie sheet at 375 degrees until light brown.

PEANUT BUTTER COOKIES   Mom

1 cup peanut butter
1 cup brown sugar
1 cup sugar
1 cup shortening
2 eggs
2 ½ cups flour
1 tsp soda
1 tsp baking powder
1 tsp salt

Bake 10-12 minutes at 375 degrees.

PEANUT BUTTER COOKIES   **Grandma Erb**

½ cup butter or shortening
1 cup brown sugar

1 cup white sugar
¾ to 1 cup peanut butter
2 eggs
2 tsp soda
3-4 cups flour

Mix first four ingredients. Add eggs, mixing well. Roll in ball, dip in sugar, and flatten with fork crisscrossed. Add dry ingredients. Bake at 350 degrees on greased sheets until brown.

POWDERED SUGAR COOKIES   Grandma Erb

1 cup each powdered sugar & shortening
1 tsp each soda & cream of tartar
1 tsp vanilla
1 egg, beaten
2½ cup flour
Mix as pie dough.

PUMPKIN COOKIES   Mom

2 cups brown sugar, packed firmly
2 cups cooked or canned pumpkin
1 cup salad oil
2 tsp vanilla
4 cup sifted flour
2 tsp soda
2 tsp baking powder
1 tsp each salt, cinnamon & nutmeg
½ tsp ginger
2 cups raisins
1 cup chopped nuts

In mixing bowl, beat together sugar, pumpkin, oil and vanilla. Soft together dry ingredients, add and stir until smooth. Blend in raisins and nuts. Drop by spoonfuls on oiled baking sheets. Bake at 350 degrees for 12-15 minutes. Makes about 7 dozen.

RITZ CRACKERS COOKIES   Ruth Ann

1 pkg crackers
1 pkg dates
1 can sweetened condensed milk

Cut up dates and cook with milk, stirring constantly for 5 minutes on low temperature. Put between crackers and bake 5 minutes. Frost with 3 oz cream cheese, 2 ½ cup powdered sugar, 4 Tbsp margarine, and 1 tsp vanilla.

SIX IN ONE OATMEAL COOKIES   Grandma Erb

1 cup shortening
1 cup brown sugar
2 eggs
1 tsp vanilla
1 tsp soda
3 cups quick oats
1½ cups flour
1 tsp salt

Cream shortening & sugar. Add eggs and vanilla and beat. Add dry ingredients. Then add one of the following:
½ cup chopped nuts
1 pkg chocolate chips
2 Tbsp grated orange peel
1 cup raisins
1 cup chopped dates
1 cup shredded coconut

Bake at 375 degrees.

SNICKERDOODLES   Paul

1 cup soft shortening, part butter
1 ½ cup sugar
2 eggs
2¾ cup flour
2 tsp cream of tartar
1 tsp soda
¼ tsp salt

Heat oven to 400 degrees. Mix shortening, sugar and eggs thoroughly. Measure flour into bowl. Blend all dry ingredients; stir in. Roll into balls the size of small walnuts. Roll in mixture of 2 Tbsp sugar and 2 tsp cinnamon. Place 2" apart on ungreased baking sheet. Bake 8-10 minutes. (These cookies puff up at first, then flatten out.) Makes about 5 dozen.

SPARKLING GINGERSNAPS   Mom

1 cup sugar
½ cup shortening
¼ cup light molasses
¼ cup butter
1 egg
2 cups flour
1 ½ tsp soda
1 tsp cinnamon
½ tsp each salt, ginger, allspice

Mix, roll in ball, then roll in sugar. Place 2 ½" apart on ungreased sheet. Bake at 350 degrees 12 minutes or until tops crack. Cool briefly. Lift onto rack. Puffed cookies flatten as they cool. 6 dozen.

SUGAR COOKIES   Grandma Erb

1 cup shortening
2 cups sugar
4 eggs
¼ cup cream
¼ tsp vanilla or mace
2 tsp baking powder
1 tsp soda
3 ½ cups flour

Cream shortening and sugar. Add eggs one at a time and beat. Ad cream and sifted dry ingredients. Chill overnight. Roll and bake.

WAGON WHEEL COOKIES   Mom

2 cups sugar
4 eggs
2 tsp vanilla
½ cup melted shortening
4 sq. melted chocolate
2 cups flour
2 tsp baking powder
1 tsp salt
½ cup chopped walnuts

Beat eggs with sugar and vanilla; blend in melted chocolate and shortening. Sift dry ingredients together, stir into mixture. Add walnuts. Chill several hours or overnight. Shape into balls, roll in powdered sugar and place on ungreased cookie sheet about 2 inches apart. Bake in 350 oven 10 –15 min or until done. (Remove from oven before they look done for a moist chewy cookie.) Makes 4 dozen.

WASHBOARD COOKIES   Great Aunt Mary Erb
(Dad's Aunt)

2 cups brown sugar
1 cup fat (half butter and half oleo is good)
2 eggs
3¾ cup flour
2 tsp soda
¼ tsp salt
2 tsp cream of tartar
1 tsp vanilla
1 cup coconut

Bake at 375 degrees.

Uncle Jim, holding Ron, Aunt Verda

DESSERTS

ALMOND CHEESECAKE — Theresa/Sheila

CRUST:
1 ¼ cups crushed vanilla wafers
¾ cup finely chopped almonds
¼ cup sugar
1/3 cup melted butter

FILLING:
4 pkgs (8 oz each) cream cheese, softened
1 ¼ cups sugar
4 eggs
1 ½ tsp almond extract
1 tsp vanilla extract

TOPPING:
2 cups (16 oz) sour cream
¼ cup sugar
1 tsp vanilla extract
1/8 cup toasted sliced almonds

In a bowl, combine wafers, almonds, and sugar; add the butter and mix well. Press into the bottom on an ungreased 10 inch spring form pan; set aside. In a large mixing bowl, beat cream cheese and sugar until creamy. Add eggs, one at a time, beating well after each addition. Add extracts; beat just until blended. Pour into crust. Bake at 350 degrees for 55 minutes or until center is almost set. Remove from the oven; let stand for 5 minutes. Combine sour cream, sugar and vanilla; spread over filling. Return to the oven for 5 minutes. Cool on a wire rack; chill overnight. Just before serving, sprinkle with almonds and remove sides of pan. Store in refrigerator. Serves 14-16.

APPLE DUMPLINGS   Ruth Ann

1 cup brown sugar
2 cups water
3 Tbsp butter
¼ tsp cinnamon
Boil these ingredients for 3 minutes.

Make pie dough and roll out. Take core out of apple and place dough around each apple. Place in glass cake pan-6 apples. Mix ½ cup brown sugar, 1 ½ tsp cinnamon, 1 Tbsp butter and put down into center of apples. Pour boiled mixture into pan, around apples and bake 40-45 minutes at 425 degrees. Serve hot with whipped cream. These are always a big hit.

APPLE PUDDING   Grandma Erb

6 large apples
2 eggs
¾ cups sugar
1 tsp cinnamon
¼ cup shortening
½ cup water
1 cup flour
1 tsp baking powder
1 tsp salt

Pare and slice apples. Mix with sugar and cinnamon. Place in a greased pan. In another dish, place beaten eggs, salt, and shortening. Mix. Add flour, baking powder and water. Pour over apples. Bake at 350 degrees for one half hour.

BUSTER BAR DESSERT — Sheila

2 cups powdered sugar
1 can evaporated milk
2/3 cup chocolate chips
½ cup margarine or butter
1 tsp vanilla
1 8 oz or larger Cool Whip
1 lb. Oreo cookies, crushed
½ cup melted margarine or butter
1 ½ cup Spanish peanuts
½ gal. vanilla ice cream, softened

Heat first four ingredients in pan. Boil 8 minutes, stirring constantly. Cool and add vanilla. Mix crushed cookies and melted butter. Spread in a 9x13 pan. Pour peanuts over cookie mixture and refrigerate. When set, put softened ice cream over peanuts. Cover with chocolate chip mixture. Put Cool Whip over chocolate. Sprinkle a few more peanuts on top. Freeze overnight.

It may be of interest to you to know that the original Buster Bar from DQ was created in the 1960's by Mr. Munson, the owner of the Park Rapids Dairy Queen.

FRUIT COCKTAIL DESSERT — Grandma Erb

1 can fruit cocktail
1 cup sugar
1 cup flour
1 tsp soda
¼ tsp salt
1 beaten egg

Mix sugar, flour, soda, salt & egg. Add fruit cocktail and stir. Combine the following and put on top:

½ cup brown sugar
½ cup chopped nuts
Bake about an hour in slow oven.

ICE CREAM   Mom

½ cup sugar
¼ tsp salt
1 cup milk
2 egg yolks, beaten
1 Tbsp vanilla
1 cup whipping cream

Blend sugar, salt, milk and egg yolks in saucepan. Cook over medium heat, stirring constantly, just until mixture comes to a boil. Cool. Add vanilla and whipping cream. Freeze according to directions on freezer.

ICE CREAM   Theresa

2 ¼ cups sugar
¼ cup plus 2 Tbsp flour
½ tsp salt
5 cups milk
4 beaten eggs
4 cups whipping cream
2 Tbsp vanilla

Combine sugar, flour, and salt in pan. Gradually stir in milk. Cook over medium heat 15 minutes or until thickened, stirring constantly. Gradually stir 1 cup hot mixture into eggs. Add to remaining mixture, stirring constantly. Cook 1 minute. Remove from heat. Refrigerate 2 hours. Add mixture, cream and vanilla. Mix well and freeze according to freezer directions.

LEMON REFRIGERATOR DESSERT   Mom
(Mom made this often when we were kids.)

Combine:
2 egg yolks, slightly beaten
1/3 cup sugar
2 Tbsp lemon juice
½ tsp grated lemon rind

Cook in double boiler until thick, stirring constantly. Cool. Beat 2 eggs whites until stiff. Add 2 Tbsp sugar, gradually. Fold meringue into lemon filling. Fold in 2/3 cup heavy cream, whipped. Cover shallow freezing tray with ¼ cup vanilla wafer crumbs. Pour filling over crumbs and top with ¼ cup more vanilla wafer crumbs. Freeze. Cut in wedges to serve.

PECAN BAR DESSERT   Diane

Butter a 9x13 pan. Mix, crumble, and put in pan:
2 ½ cups flour
½ cup sugar
½ tsp salt
1 cup cold butter

Bake 20-25 minutes until golden brown. While baking, beat:
4 eggs
1 ½ cups sugar
3 Tbsp melted butter
1 ½ tsp vanilla
Stir in:
2 ½ cup pecans

Pour over hot crust. Spread evenly and bake 25 minutes till firm around edges and slightly firm in center. Serve with whipped cream flavored with vanilla and almond.

PUMPKIN DESSERT　　　　　　　**Rozanne**

1 large can pumpkin
4 eggs
1 ½ cups sugar
¼ tsp salt
1 ½ tsp each cloves, cinnamon, and ginger

Mix and pour into a 9x13 pan. Sprinkle dry yellow cake mix on top. Melt 2 sticks margarine. Pour over cake mix. Cover with pecans. Bake about one hour at 350 degrees.

PUMPKIN PIE SQUARES　　　　**Aunt Verda**

1 cup flour
½ cup quick oatmeal
½ cup packed brown sugar
½ cup butter
2 cup pumpkin, cooked or canned
1 (13 ½ oz.) can evaporated milk
2 eggs
¾ cup sugar
½ tsp salt
½ tsp cinnamon
½ tsp ginger
¼ tsp cloves
½ cup chopped nuts
½ cup packed brown sugar
2 Tbsp butter

Combine flour, oats, ½ cup brown sugar and ½ cup butter.

Mix until crumbly. Press into 9x13 pan. Bake at 350 degrees for 15 minutes. Combine pumpkin, milk, eggs, sugar, salt and spices in bowl. Bet well. Pour into crust and bake at 350 degrees for 30 minutes. Combine nuts, ½ cup brown sugar and 2 Tbsp butter. Sprinkle over pumpkin filling, return to oven and bake 15-20 minutes or until filling is set. Top with Cool Whip.

RASPBERRY DESSERT   **Mom**
(Originally from friend, LaMae James)

Cook until thick:
2 – 10 oz packages frozen raspberries
1 cup water
½ cup sugar
2 tsp lemon juice
4 Tbsp cornstarch in ½ cup cold water

Cool. Melt 50 large marshmallows and 1 cup milk. Cool. Fold into 2 cups cream, whipped or 2 packages Dream Whip.
Mix:
1 ½ cups graham cracker crumbs (about 9 double crackers)
½ cup nuts
½ cup melted butter

Press down in 9x13 inch pan. Add marshmallow mixture. Then raspberry mixture. Then chill.

RHUBARB SAUCE

3 cups rhubarb, chopped
1 cup sugar

Bring to a boil. Cook until rhubarb is done. May need to add more sugar. Or, you may add 2 Tbsp red jello (wild strawberry is especially good). Cool.

STICKY CHOCOLATE TOPPING   Mom

¼ cup butter
¼ cup cocoa
¼ cup milk
1 cup sugar

Slowly bring to a boil over low heat. Boil one minute, take off heat and add one tsp vanilla. Cool slightly. This can also be used as frosting. Cool to lukewarm and beat to a spreading consistency. (Grandma Erb's frosting recipe.)

SWEET RICE   Grandma Erb

1 cup rice
2 cups water
Milk
1 cup sugar
Raisins, cooked (optional)

Cook rice in water until all is absorbed, then add 1 cup sugar and milk just to cover rice. Cook over low heat until thickened. Cool. May add cooked raisins, if desired.

WHITE CHOCOLATE RASPBERRY CHEESECAKE
Rozanne

Crust:
1 ¼ cup finely ground shortbread cookie crumbs
¼ cup ground almonds (about 1 oz.)
2 Tbsp sugar
1/8 tsp almond extract
3 Tbsp melted butter
Preheat oven to 350 degrees. Mix first 4 ingredients in small bowl. Blend in butter. Press in bottom of 10" spring form pan. Bake 10 minutes. Transfer to rack and cool completely. Reduce oven to 325 degrees.

Filling:
6 oz white chocolate (preferably imported) – finely chopped
4 – 8 oz pkgs cream cheese, room temperature
5 eggs, room temperature
¾ cup sugar
3 Tbsp flour
1 tsp vanilla
¼ tsp almond extract
Melt chocolate until smooth; cool to lukewarm. Beat cheese until smooth; add eggs, 1 at a time. Mix in sugar, flour, and flavorings. Stir one cup mixture into lukewarm chocolate mixture. Add to remaining filling and sir until smooth. Pour filling in crust and bake until firm around edges and slightly set in center, about 40 minutes. Cool completely on rack. Cover and refrigerate overnight. (Rosy baked it 50 minutes.)

Glaze:
7 Tbsp whipping cream
8 oz finely chopped white chocolate
¼ cup raspberry jam, melted and strained
Toasted sliced almonds
Fresh berries, optional
1 –12 oz bag frozen unsweetened raspberries, thawed,

pureed & strained
Bring cream to a simmer in pan over low heat. Add chocolate and stir till smooth. Spoon over cheesecake. Using spatula, spread lightly over edge. Refrigerate until set. (Rosy said ½ amount of ingredients in enough.). Brush jam around sides of cheesecake. Press almonds into sides covering completely. Drop some of jam on top. (Can be prepared 2 days ahead. Cover and refrigerate.) Arrange fresh raspberries in center, if desired. Serve with raspberry puree.

YULETIDE CHOCOLATE DESSERT **Mom**
(This was served at the baby shower for Kimmy.)

2 cups vanilla wafer crumbs
1/3 cup melted butter
Mix and save 2 Tbsp. Put rest in 9x13 inch pan.
½ cup butter
1 ½ cup powdered sugar
2 eggs
Cream butter and sugars. Then add eggs, 1 at a time. Spread over crumbs.
1 cup cream, whipped
¼ cup sugar
2 Tbsp cocoa
1 ripe banana, mashed
¼ cup maraschino cherries
1 cup chopped walnuts
Fold together and put in pan. Crumbs on top. Freeze.

Erb Family Cookbook

Diane, Theresa, Sheila, Paul, Dad, Kim

Paul, Rozanne, Theresa, Sheila, Diane

Erb Family Cookbook

Dear Grandma,

As I was assembling this cookbook, I thought about you so much. My heart warms each time I remember what a wonderful Grandmother you were. I have many wonderful memories of you; like your smiling face, and how I knew you loved me no matter what; the way you would hold my hand, with your thumb gently rubbing my fingers; the way you patiently taught me to crochet; eating pancakes while we sat on your front porch; and how happy you were for me when I married my sweetheart. Remember how we stopped in to see you right after the wedding?

Then I had a flashback to the first time you came to visit us in our own little home. I wanted to make something special and so we decided on homemade ice cream. Now remember, I hadn't been married too long and hadn't made homemade ice cream too often. But I read up on it and with my new ice cream maker I set to work. It said to make it ahead and "cure" it awhile. So I did that. We made it before you and Mom and Dad came out. After it was done, I removed the dasher, packed it down and put the lid back on. We put some more ice around it, put a towel on top of it and set it out on the front step in the wintery cold to "cure".

You arrived just a little later, with Mom and Dad, and in you all came. I took you through my house and showed it all to you. I was so proud to have a little home of my own. I always wanted to be just like you, you know, with a little house and family to love and take care of. After awhile of sitting in the living room and talking, I decided it was time for ice cream. I went out to the front step and was horrified! There the lid was off the ice cream maker, the towel gone (heaven only knew where) and the ice cream was being sampled and enjoyed by the big white mutt named Buster! Boy, did I want to "bust" his chops!

    I carried the bucket inside, so disheartened by what had happened. We all looked over the damage and decided that it wasn't that bad. Buster had barely gotten into it, so it was suggested that we scoop off the top few inches and eat it. You were very gracious about the whole thing and made me feel like I was treating you like a queen. Such a queen, to eat ice cream the dog had slobbered in! It was just another example of what a wonderful grandmother you were.

    There's a scripture in the Bible from the book of Titus, referred to as the "Titus woman". You certainly were that in your life and I am so proud to be your granddaughter. I wish you would have known my daughter and son and they would have known you and the blessing you were. I pray one day, God willing, I can be to my grandchildren the loving grandmother you were to us, your grandchildren.

    I love you and miss you, Grandma,
                    Theresa

Erb Family Cookbook

"Likewise, teach the older women to be reverent in the way they live, not to be slanderers or addicted to much wine, but to teach what is good. Then they can train the younger women to love their husbands and children, to be self-controlled and pure, to be busy at home, to be kind, and to be subject to their husbands, so that no one will malign the word of God." Titus 2:3-5 (NIV)

Grandma Erb (1977)

Grandma Erb (at Wayne & Theresa's weddiing in 1978)

MAIN COURSES

BAR-B-Q HAMBURGERS   Grandma Erb

2 lbs. hamburger
2 onions
2 tsp each dry mustard & chili powder
2 tsp salt
½ tsp pepper
½ cup ketchup
Put in skillet, over low heat and cook till done. Stir often.

BEAN HOTDISH   Theresa

Brown 1 lb hamburger and several strips of bacon (diced). Add:
1 can pork & beans
1 can chili hot beans
1 can red kidney beans
1 cup brown sugar
1 cup ketchup
1 large onion, chopped

Bake at 350 degrees for 45 minutes, uncovered.

CHICKEN BREAST PARMESAN   Sue

Combine the following three ingredients:
1/3 cup corn flakes, crushed
¼ cup Parmesan cheese
1 tsp dried parsley flakes

1 beaten egg
2 large chicken breasts
1 can Spaghetti Sauce
Dip chicken in egg and then in corn flake mixture. Place on cookie Sheet. Bake for about 25-35 minutes at 350 degrees. Pull out and pour sauce on top of each piece and sprinkle with mozzarella cheese. Place back in oven for 10 minutes to melt cheese and heat sauce.

CHICKEN NOODLE CASSEROLE   Aunt Verda

1 chicken cooked and boned
1 can mushroom soup
salt
¼ cup grated American cheese
1 - 8 oz pkg noodles
1 cup milk
2 Tbsp butter

Cook noodles in salted boiling water, drain. Put layer of noodles in greased baking dish, add layer of chicken and half of cheese, top with another layer of noodles, chicken and cheese. Mix soup and milk and pour over noodles, dot with butter and bake at 375 degrees for 30 minutes. Add a little chicken broth for added flavor.

DRESSING FOR TURKEY OR CHICKEN   Mom

Cook giblets in water to cover, with 1 chopped onion, salt and pepper. After tender, cool and chop meat, save broth. (Liver cooks fast so take it out in a little while.)
Simmer 1 cup chopped onion in ¼ cup melted butter very slowly until transparent. Add another ¼ cup butter, 2 cups milk, 1 cup cream, the giblets and broth. Heat a little till butter melts.
Pour above mixture over 8 cups broken dry bread. Stir.

Let set a little to soften bread. Add 4 eggs and mix well. Add more milk, cream, or bread to make desired consistency. Also salt and pepper to taste. (You can taste it to see you don't get too much salt because some ingredients already have salt in them.)

Put dressing very loosely in fowl as it swells as it cooks. Put any leftover dressing on outside of turkey at one end of roaster (or in a separate dish). I put dressing in fowl about 2 hours before end of roasting time, bake uncovered first hour and then cover loosely the last hour.

When you put dressing in bowl to serve it is good to take some of the juices from the roaster and place over dressing and mix just a little.

All of the ingredients are approximate measures. Add more or less of anything to suit your taste.

FRIED CHICKEN   **Mom**

Dip cut up chicken in flour in bowl and put in hot skillet with shortening melted in it. Fry until brown, then turn. Salt and pepper. When second side is browned, turn and salt and pepper again. Continue to turn and fry until done, lowering heat. You may cover with a lid and steam part of the time. To get it crispy again, you must remove the lid and fry until crispy.

To make gravy:
Remove chicken from pan. Sprinkle flour into drippings in pan, having heat on low. Stir the flour into the drippings until absorbed nicely. Add milk slowly to frying pan and continue to cook and add milk until desired consistency. Salt and pepper. Let boil gently until ready. Also good if you use part potato water in place of some of the milk.

HOT DISH   **Aunt Jeannie**

1 ½ lb hamburger (browned with onion)
½ lb bacon (fry till crisp and crumble)
1 can kidney beans
1 can pork & beans
1 can lima beans (drained)
1/3 cup brown sugar
1/3 cup ketchup
1/3 cup Heinz barbeque sauce

Mix all together. Bake 1 hour at 350 degrees.

MARINATED CHICKEN BREASTS   **Sue**

6 chicken breasts, skinned and boned
1/3 cup olive oil
3 cloves garlic, crushed
1 ½ Tbsp lemon juice
1 ½ Tbsp lime juice
¼ tsp pepper
½ cup firmly packed brown sugar
¼ cup cider vinegar
3 Tbsp course grain prepared mustard
1 ½ tsp salt

Place chicken in large zippered plastic bag. Combine the rest of the ingredients and mix well. Pour over chicken and let marinate 4 hours or more. (Sue puts hers in the night before). Discard juice and grill chicken 8 minutes on each side.

MEATBALLS   Theresa

3 lbs hamburger
2 cups quick oatmeal
2 eggs
½ tsp garlic powder
2 tsp salt
1 chopped onion (or ¼ cup dry onion flakes)
½ tsp pepper
1 Tbsp chili powder

Mix and form into balls about the size of a golf ball. Put in single layer in baking dish.

Sauce:
2 cups ketchup
2 Tbsp liquid smoke
½ cup chopped onion or 2 Tbsp dry onion flakes
1 cup brown sugar
½ tsp garlic salt

Mix and pour over meatballs in pan. Bake 1 hour at 350 degrees. Meatballs freeze well and can be baked later.

MEAT LOAF (that will slice)   Grandma Erb

1 ½ lb. ground beef
¾ cup oatmeal
2 beaten eggs
1 cup tomato juice
2 tsp salt
¼ cup chopped onion
½ tsp pepper

Combine all ingredients. Pack firmly in loaf pan. Bake 350 degrees 1 hour. Let stand 5 minutes before slicing.

MEXICAN FIESTA   **Mom**

Meat sauce:
4 lbs ground beef
2-3 medium chopped onions
2 – 16 oz cans tomatoes
15 oz tomato sauce
2 large cans tomato paste
3 Tbsp chili powder
1 clove garlic, minced
2 large cans Ranch style (pinto) beans
Cook 3 hours the day before and allow to set and flavors to blend. Reheat to serve.
Pile on in order and don't skip any!
1. Crushed Fritos
2. Cooked rice (can use 3 minute)
3. Meat sauce
4. Grated cheese
5. Lettuce and tomato
6. Chopped olives, black or green
7. Chopped pecans
8. Shredded coconut
9. Picante sauce

May add sour cream on top.

(Mom originally got this recipe from Sue, Paul's wife, who got it from Paul's cousin Merlyn's wife, Dee.)

PENNSYLVANIA SCRAPPLE

2 cups cornmeal
1 ½ lbs cooked chopped pork
½ tsp salt
¼ tsp pepper
1 onion, minced
flour

4 Tbsp butter

Bring 2 qts water to a boil. Slowly add cornmeal and cook until thick, stirring constantly. Add pork, seasonings, and onion; continue cooking for 10 minutes. Rinse a shallow oblong pan with cold water; pour mixture into pan. Refrigerate overnight. Cut scrapple in slices; dip in flour. Heat butter in heavy skillet. Fry on both sides until golden brown.

SAUERKRAUT HOTDISH **Aunt Verda**

Brown 2 pounds hamburger with 1 chopped onion. Layer half of beef mix in 9x13 baking dish. Cover with 1 qt sauerkraut and top with remaining hamburger. Put 4 cups uncooked wide egg noodles on top. Mix 2 cans cream of celery and 2 cans of cream of mushroom soup together and spread over noodles and bake 30 minutes at 350 degrees. Take out and sprinkle 2 cups cheddar cheese on top. Bake for another 30 minutes or until cheese starts to brown.

SHRIMP CREOLE **Sue**

1 ½ lb shrimp
2 Tbsp bacon grease
3 cloves garlic, chopped
1 Tbsp crushed peppercorn
1 large onion, sliced
5 stalks celery, cut diagonally
1 Tbsp Creole seasoning
1 large can tomatoes, drained & chopped
1 large can mushrooms
1 Tbsp chopped parsley
2 dashes Tabasco Sauce (about 6 shakes)
Salt and pepper to taste

1 Tbsp lemon Juice
pinch Marjoram
1 Tbsp Accent
2 cans tomato soup, undiluted
½ cup sherry

Sauté onions, celery pepper, garlic in bacon drippings until soft (15 minutes). Add all of the other ingredients and simmer 30 minutes or more-very low temp. Add shrimp 20 minutes before serving. DO NOT THAW SHRIMP. Serve over rice.
Note: Sue likes to make it the day before so the flavors blend and then she adds the shrimp after she's heated it and cooks for 20 minutes.

SPAGHETTI SAUCE   **Diane**

2 large tomato sauces
3 tomato pastes
1 can spaghetti sauce
1 qt tomatoes
1 small head cabbage, chopped
3-4 onions, chopped fine
mushrooms
2 carrots, chopped
1 Tbsp each basil and oregano
¼ cup lemon juice
1 head garlic, minced

Cook all together for several hours.

TACORETTOS **Aunt Jeannie**

Flour taco shells
Refried beans, heat with a little water
Chopped tomatoes
Chopped onions
Chopped lettuce
3 lbs hamburger, browned with 1 pkg dry taco seasoning
Grated cheddar cheese
Grated mozzarella cheese

Layer taco shell with ½" beans, tomatoes, onions, lettuce, hamburger, cheddar cheese, mozzarella cheese, another taco shell, and then another layer of each thing listed. Bake ½ hour at 350 to 375 degrees. (Put 2 on a cookie sheet.) Serve with hot sauce.

TUNA SANDWICHES **Mom**

Mix tuna and miracle whip. Spread thinly between 2 slices of bread. Cut in half. May add chopped onion.

Erb Family Cookbook
To Grandmother's House We Go

It was Thanksgiving Day and the Erb Family was on their way to Grandma and Grandpa Erb's for dinner. As usual, Diane, Paul, Rozanne, and Sheila sat in the back seat of the car. Dad was driving, with Theresa in between he and Mom, and Kimmy sat on Mom's lap. It was a sort of long ride for kids Theresa's age. Long enough for a nap, especially on the way home, when she was full and warm.

The weather was pretty nice for November, clear and cold. There had been a few inches of snow 3 days ago, so everything was sparkly white in the sun, but the roads were clear for all the holiday travelers.

They had just gone through Osage, passing Doc's Café. It was a nice little café; a place where Grandma and Grandpa loved to stop for coffee when they came to visit the Erbs on their farm. Mom said they had a pretty good pumpkin pie at the café, but Theresa loved Aunt Verda's pumpkin pie and couldn't imagine any better. She was looking forward to that pie today, smothered with whipped cream. M-m-m-m-m! Her mouth watered just thinking of it.

Mom turned in the seat and said to the group at large, "Everybody be on your best behavior today. Play nice together and eat what's on your plate."

Dad chuckled. "Yes," he said, "whatever's there you eat. When I was a kid and we'd go to someone's house for a meal, we always ate whatever we were served, whether we liked it or not. I can remember many occasions when we would have baked beans and I'd find a little rock in them that the cook had missed when cleaning the beans. We just swallowed it down, because kids were seen and not heard in those days, and it would have been impolite to the cook to say anything. We never really wanted anyone to notice us anyhow."

"Yuck," Theresa said.

"Yeah," said Dad, "it wasn't too good, but hair was worse. I've swallowed many a piece of hair in food because we'd been told not to say anything at the table or to make a scene."

O-o-o! Theresa could just imagine a piece of hair stuck in her mouth. She didn't know if she could just swallow it or not. But she'd try not to be an embarrassment to her folks. Maybe she could discreetly take it out. O-o-o! She shuddered just thinking of it.

Diane said, "I can't wait for those great buns that Grandma makes."

Grandma made a wonderful little bun that was light and airy and loved by all.

"When we were kids, we didn't always have much food," said Dad. "There were a lot of kids and times were hard. For something special, Grandma would take little pieces of bread when she baked and make them into rolls. Then she would take her thumb and punch a little hole part way into them. After they baked she would put just a little bit of jelly into the hole. We thought we were eating the food of kings!"

Theresa could just imagine her Dad and his brothers sitting together eating those nice little rolls with crowns on their heads. It made her smile.

Her parents often told stories about their childhoods and she always loved to hear them. They made her feel warm inside, thinking of her parents as children like herself.

Beside her, Dad started to hum "How Great Thou Art". When he got to the chorus he started to sing and by the time he got to the second line of the chorus, Diane had started to sing along in alto, making a wonderful contrast to Dad's melody. Theresa sat back and enjoyed. Once in a while she could hear one of the other girls sing a line or so, but mostly it was Dad and Diane. She closed her eyes…

*****

As they parked along the street at Grandma and Grandpa's, Theresa noticed there were already a lot of cars in the driveway and along the street on both sides. She wondered if everyone was coming to Grandma's for Thanksgiving Dinner.

They piled out. It seemed they each had something to carry. Grandma made the turkey and fixings and all the aunts brought some food to share. Today Mom brought a pecan pie and a hot bean salad. Dad opened the trunk and plucked the pie out, giving it to Diane and carrying the salad himself. Paul reached in the trunk for a brown paper bag with the kids' outside clothes in it and Rosy carried Kimmy's diaper bag. Sheila had some books and Theresa had a box of crayons and a coloring book. Mom carried Kimmy.

The door was opened before they got there. Mary, (Mabel and Rome's youngest daughter) stood there with a smiling face, and said, "Hi, Rose!" She was closest to Rozanne's age and of course, as with most of the cousins, she was *closest* to Rozanne. Theresa was used to being left out, but today she thought Sheila would probably play with her, as most of the cousins were there and they would take the "popular" Rozanne and leave the other two out.

Inside people were EVERYWHERE.

Grandma's house didn't seem that small, but with so many children and grandchildren inside it was packed. The smells were wonderful. People began to take the food items and pass them along to the kitchen while Theresa's family took off their coats, hats and other outerwear in the entry. Then single file they went between the lines of people into the kitchen, stopping to say hello to various ones along the way. Theresa smiled at her cousin Merlyn as she passed him. He was several years older than her; a teenage in fact. He was very shy but always polite to her. Someone said, "My how you've grown!" and patted her on the head, but she was pushed along through the throng without seeing who it was.

  In the kitchen, Grandma hugged each newcomer and took Kimmy in her arms to squeeze her a little extra. Everybody loved Kimmy. She was such a smiling, sweet thing. Theresa didn't think anyone could resist her.

  Grandma had set up a long table the length of the living room that came just into the kitchen. The plates and silverware were all in place and it looked so nice with the tablecloth and all. The big table in the kitchen was set and ready also. Theresa found a place by the upstairs door, and kind of tucked herself in by the heater in the living room. She stood and just looked around at everyone. At the moment looking and talking was all there seemed to be room for. The men congregated on the chairs and sofa around the outside of the living room and the women stayed in the kitchen to help Grandma should she need it. Theresa had lost sight of Rose and Mary, but Sheila stood behind Dad, who had Kimmy on his lap and was talking to the uncles while he sat in the rocking chair.

Grandpa smiled at her from across the room as she looked his way. She liked Grandpa but she was a little afraid of him for some reason. Maybe because of the stories Dad told about how strong he was. Once he lifted the front end of a car just so the tire could be changed. Looking at Grandpa now, she didn't think he looked like someone who could lift a car but he was old now. In his sixties, which to Theresa was *very* old.

    Suddenly there was a shriek from the kitchen. "Mom's hair's on fire!" someone yelled and it seemed to be mass confusion. Theresa couldn't see what happened, but it was all over about as fast as it happened. When everyone was back in their place, Theresa slowly went into the kitchen to check on Grandma. Grandma was laughing! She saw Theresa's worried face first thing and put her arm around her. "I'm fine," she said. "I bent over to check the turkey in the oven and got my hair a little too close to the burner where the gravy was cooking." Theresa could see the burned off hairs on the front of Grandma's head and it smelt a little funny in the kitchen. "I'm such a silly," Grandma said, laughing again as she bent to kiss Theresa on the top of her head. "Back to work," she said and went on with her dinner preparations as if she caught her hair on fire every time she cooked.

*****

    Because the Erb family had grown to be so many, there wasn't any way they could all sit and eat together at one time, so it had become the custom to feed the kids first and then the women would wash up the dishes and all of the adults would sit down and eat.

As the food was passed around Theresa put the different things on her plate. Knowing she would have to eat whatever she took, she was careful to take only the things she was pretty sure she would like. The tricky part was trying to tell if there were any hairs in anything, but she finally figured she'd just have to take a chance on some of it, because it all looked pretty good. She looked up from her plate at her brother, Paul, who was sitting across the table by some of the boy cousins. She noticed he was passing the cranberry salad on without taking any. Everyone knew Paul didn't like cranberries. Theresa wasn't sure she liked them that well either, but this time there was a salad that Grandma had made with ground cranberries and jello and other fruit, so Theresa thought she would try just a little. It was pretty tasty! Paul might even like it, but then again, maybe not. He held pretty firm to his rule of no cranberries.

After her pumpkin pie, Theresa was full. She got down from her chair and looked for Sheila to do something with. Sheila was playing with Kimmy. Mom had fed Kimmy while the kids ate and was now ready to sit down and eat her dinner. Theresa walked in the living room and looked in the little glass doored cabinet that Grandma had there. She could see Mary's little pair of eyeglasses inside and thought sadly about Dad's little sister, Mary, who had died when she was just two. On the wall hung a large picture of what Theresa always thought was a boat coming into the harbor. Today she looked at it closely and realized it wasn't a boat at all. It was a picture of a long table with a blue cloth and dishes sitting around the edges. It was different than most pictures as it was close to you at the front and seemed to get further away in the back. Theresa looked again and couldn't believe that she had always thought that it was a boat. She had never really looked that closely before.

    The adults were laughing and eating and the kids were pretty much gone. When the tables were cleared Theresa thought she would bring out her colors and coloring book. She loved to color and was very good at it. Mom always praised her for her good work. But she'd have to wait a bit for that.

    Theresa noticed that Sheila had taken Kimmy into Grandma's bedroom to play with her and so she decided to go in and see if she could help.

*****

    They had packed up all the things they'd brought and were pulling away from the curb at Grandma's. Theresa was tired. Not from overplaying with a bunch of cousins all different ages. No, she had pretty much played by herself or with Sheila. But all of the commotion and being full made her feel a little sleepy. Kimmy sat quiet on Mom's lap. Theresa rested her head against Dad's arm, feeling comfortable and safe. Dad and Mom were talking.

"Mabel's Scalloped Corn was really good," Mom said. It was the first time it had been served and Mom had really liked it.

"Yes, it was. And there's nothing like a piece of Grandma's Apple Pie. Did you hear Jim say he'd shot a bear?"

Their voices went back and forth discussing the day's events. Theresa's eyes got heavy and she found herself getting sleepier and sleepier. The last thing she thought she heard was Dad saying, "...and no hair in it either."

Mom and Theresa on her first birthday

PIES

APPLE PIE   **Grandma Erb**

Peel 5-6 baking apples and slice into an unbaked pie crust.
Mix:
1 cup sugar
1/3 cup flour
1 cup cream
Pour over apples in pie plate. Pour more cream on top to cover nicely. Sprinkle top with cinnamon. Bake at 375 degrees until apples are tender and filling is set, approximately 1 hour. Cool. Best served cold.

BANANA CREAM PIE   Mom

½ cup sugar
½ tsp salt
2 Tbsp cornstarch
1 Tbsp flour
2 cups milk
2 egg yolks
½ Tbsp butter
1 tsp vanilla

Mix sugar, salt, cornstarch and flour in top of double boiler. Stir in milk. Bring to a boil over low heat, and boil 3 minutes, stirring constantly. Remove from heat. Stir a little of the hot mixture into slightly beaten egg yolks…then blend all into hot mixture. Place over boiling water and cook 10 minutes, stirring occasionally. Blend in butter. Cool thoroughly. Blend in vanilla. Add sliced bananas (3/4 cup). Pour into cooled baked pie shell. Chill pie thoroughly (1-2 hours). Top with sweetened whipped cream. May garnish top with ring of banana slices.

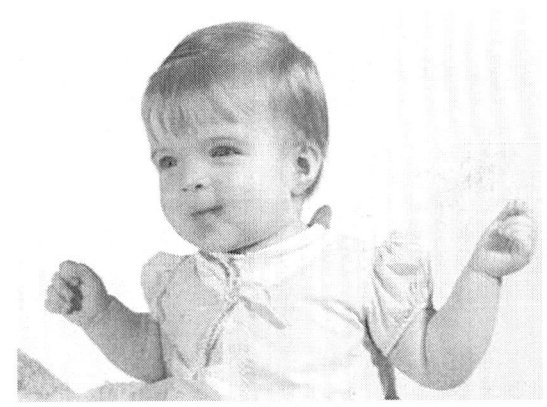

Kimberly

BUTTERSCOTCH RAISIN PIE

¾ cup raisins
1 cup water
1 cup brown sugar
2 beaten egg yolks
2 rounded Tbsp flour
Pinch of salt
1½ cup milk
1 tsp vanilla
Baked pie shell
Whipped cream

Simmer raisins and water for 10 minutes. Drain off excess liquid so you have ½ cup liquid on raisins. Mix the brown sugar, flour and salt. Add egg yolks. Beat well. Add the milk and beat well. Stir into the raisins and liquid. Cook till thick like pudding. Add vanilla. Pour into baked pie shell. Cool, top with whipped cream.

Aunt Jeannie Erb's recipe, and probably originally Grandma Erb's.

CHOCOLATE PIE   **Aunt Jeannie**

2 ½ cup milk, heat in pan
Beat 2-3 egg yolks
Mix together:
1 cup sugar,
2 very heaping Tbsp flour
2 Tbsp cocoa, barely rounded

Beat well. Add a little of the milk from the pan, beat again. Add all to milk and cook until thick-pie consistency. Add ½ tsp vanilla. Pour into baked crust. Cool.

FRENCH APPLE PIE   **Great Aunt Barb**
(Mom's Aunt)

Mix:
1 cup sugar
1/4 cup cornstarch
1/2 tsp nutmeg
1/4 tsp cinnamon
pinch of salt
Stir into 6 cups thinly sliced, tart baking apples, pared. Pour ingredients into pie pan.

Mix until crumbly:
1 cup flour
1/2 cup butter or oleo
1/2 cup brown sugar

Sprinkle topping over filling. Bake for 1 hour 30 minutes, (seems too long?) or until done. Serve warm.

GOLDEN PIE RECIPE   **Aunt Jeannie**

1 unbaked pastry shell
1 can Festal Golden Pie Pumpkin
3 eggs, slightly beaten
1 cup white sugar or light brown sugar
½ tsp salt
1 tsp cinnamon
¼ tsp cloves
¼ tsp nutmeg
¼ tsp ginger
1 cup milk or evaporated milk

Prepare a one crust pie shell. Combine eggs, sugar, salt, and spices and beat well. Blend in Festal pumpkin. Add milk and beat well. Turn into pastry lined pie pan. Bake in a hot oven (450 degrees) for 10 minutes, then reduce heat and bake at 350 degrees for 40 to 45 minutes. Pie is done when knife inserted in center comes out clean.

FRESH BLUEBERRY PIE   Sheila

1 qt blueberries
¼ cup water
1 cup sugar
2 heaping Tbsp flour

Boil 2 cups berries, water, sugar and flour until thick, stirring constantly. Remove from heat and add remaining berries. Pour into baked crust. Chill. Serve with whipped cream.

PEACHES & CREAM PIE   Theresa

Peel 4 or 5 ripe peaches, slice in an unbaked 8 or 9 inch pie shell. Mix together:
½ cup white sugar
2 Tbsp flour
¼ tsp nutmeg
dash of salt
Stir in:
½ cup cream
½ tsp vanilla

Pour over peaches. Pour another half cup of cream over top. Bake at 450 degrees 10 minutes, then 350 degrees for 40-45 minutes or until done. Good served warm or cold. (Increase measurements slightly for larger pie.)

PECAN PIE   Mom

3 eggs
2/3 cup sugar
½ tsp salt
1 cup white corn syrup
1/3 cup melted butter
1 tsp vanilla
1 cup pecans

Beat eggs, sugar, salt, butter and syrup until smooth and well blended. Stir in pecans. Pour in unbaked pie crust and bake at 375 degrees 45-60 minutes or until set. Cool.

PUMPKIN PIE   Mom
(This recipe is from Doc's Café in Osage, where Grandma & Grandpa Erb always like to stop on their way to a visit at our house in Park Rapids.)

1 cup brown sugar
1 cup Carnation milk
2 tsp cinnamon
1 tsp ginger
3 eggs
1 can (15 oz) pumpkin

PUMPKIN PIE   **Aunt Verda**
Makes one deep dish pie pan.

Combine:
¾ cup white sugar
¾ cup packed brown sugar
¾ tsp cinnamon
1½ Tbsp flour
3/8 tsp each: ginger, nutmeg, and cloves
Add:
1 (15-16 oz) can pumpkin
3 beaten eggs
½ cup cream
½ cup milk
1 unbaked pie crust
Bake 400 degrees for 15 minutes. Then turn heat down to 350 and bake 45-60 minutes.

The following makes 2 regular pie pans.

1 cup sugar
1 cup packed brown sugar
1 tsp cinnamon
2 Tbsp. flour
½ tsp each ginger, cloves and nutmeg
2½ cups pumpkin
4 beaten eggs
¾ cup milk
¾ cup cream

RAISIN CREAM PIE   **Grandma Erb**

1 cup raisins
¾ cup water
½ cup brown sugar
¼ cup butter

1 cup milk
2 Tbsp cornstarch
½ cup white sugar
2 eggs yolks
½ cup cream
¼ tsp salt
1 tsp vanilla

Boil raisins in water with lid on until tender. Add brown sugar and butter and boil a few minutes. Add milk to get hot. Mix cornstarch, white sugar, yolks and cream. Stir well and add raisin mixture. Bring to a boil. Cool slightly and add vanilla. Pour in baked shell. Make meringue with egg whites, 1 Tbsp sugar and ½ tsp vanilla. Put on pie and brown in oven.

RAISIN PIE   Grandma Erb

1 cup raisins
1 cup sugar
1 cup sour cream
1 egg, slightly beaten
1 tsp cinnamon
1 rounded Tbsp flour

Mix all together. Put in unbaked pie crust. Bake at 450 degrees for 10 minutes, then 350 degrees for 20 minutes or until done.

RASPBERRY PIE   Theresa

½ cup flour
1 cup packed brown sugar
1 cup boiling water

Mix flour and sugar. Add boiling water. Cook until thickened and smooth. Pour into the bottom of unbaked pie shell. Sprinkle 2 cups raspberries on top. Sprinkle ¼ cup white sugar on berries and pour ½ cup cream over. Bake at 375 degrees 45 minutes or until firm.

RHUBARB PIE   Grandma Erb

2 cups chopped rhubarb
1/3 cup flour
1 cup sugar
1 cup cream
1 (9") pie shell, unbaked

Fill pie shell with rhubarb. Combine sugar, flour and cream. Mix. Pour over rhubarb. Bake at 425 degrees 15 minutes. Turn heat down to 300 degrees. Continue baking for 45 minutes or until rhubarb is tender.

RHUBARB PIE   Mom

6 Tbsp margarine
1¼ cup flour
1 ½ Tbsp sugar
Mix and put in pie plate. Bake 12 minutes at 350 degrees.
Beat:
3 egg yolks
1 ½ cup sugar
6 Tbsp milk
3 Tbsp flour
Add: 3 cups chopped rhubarb. Mix well and bake 40-45 minutes or until set. Beat 3 egg whites and add ¼ cup sugar. Pour over crust and bake till brown, about 5-10 minutes.

SQUASH PIE — Sheila

1 teacup cooked squash
Pinch salt
2 eggs
1 tsp cinnamon
¼ tsp ginger
1/8 tsp nutmeg
1 cup sugar
2 Tbsp flour

Mix well, then add and mix in enough milk to fill pie shell; pour into pie shell. Bake at 425 degrees for 30 minutes or until knife comes out clean. Tastes like pumpkin, only not so strong.

STRAWBERRY PIE — Mom

Make baked pie shell of desired size.
1 qt strawberries
1 cup water
1 cup sugar
3 Tbsp cornstarch

Wash, drain and hull strawberries. Simmer 1 cup strawberries and 2/3 cup water about 3 minutes. Blend sugar, cornstarch and remaining 1/3 cup water; add to boiling mixture. Boil 1 minute, stirring constantly. Cool. Save out ½ cup choice berries; put remaining 2 ½ cups of berries in baked pie shell. Cover with cooked mixture and garnish with the ½ cup berries. Refrigerate until firm—about 2 hours. Serve with sweetened whipped cream or ice cream.

STRAWBERRY PIE   Theresa

Crust:
1½ cups flour
1 tsp salt
2 Tbsp milk
2 Tbsp sugar
½ cup vegetable oil

Combine oil and milk. Whip with fork; add flour, sugar, and salt mixture all at once. Mix lightly. Press evenly into a pie pan with fingers. Prick with fork. Bake at 350 degrees until golden, 15-20 minutes. Cool and fill.

Filling:
1 cup sugar
1 cup water
3 drops red food coloring
2 Tbsp cornstarch
4 Tbsp strawberry jello
1 qt or more berries

Combine sugar and cornstarch, then add water and food coloring. Cook until thick and clear, stirring constantly. Remove from heat; add jello and stir until dissolved. Cool slightly; add berries and put in baked, cooled crust. Chill. Serve with whipped cream.

MOM'S PIE CRUST

1/3 cup shortening (1/4 cup if using lard)
1 cup flour
¼ tsp salt
Approximately 1/3 cup cold water

Mix the shortening, flour and salt with pastry blender until the shortening is the size of peas. Add most of the cold water and mix with spoon until it all comes together in a ball. You may need to use all of the water. Put a lot of flour on the counter. Gather up the ball of dough and put on flour. Turn over to be sure both sides are well covered. Roll out to size of pie plate. *Try to handle the dough as little as possible, because rolling and re-rolling will make the dough tough.* Put the dough in the pie plate, being careful not to stretch it. Trim edges and finish them as you like (fork, crimp, etc). This makes one pie crust.

Company's Coming and Dad's Cooking!

Mom hung up the phone and turned to Dad. "That was your brother David. He and Jean and the boys are heading over. They should be here in an hour."

Dad straightened himself from the couch he'd been resting on. He'd been half dozing as he listened to the game on the TV. It was a Sunday afternoon after a very busy week. Usually Sundays were the day they all got in the car and went to visit some of the relatives in Detroit Lakes or Frazee after church and lunch. But this week had been so busy that they had decided to stay home and just rest, like the Good Book said.

Mom still stood by the phone. "Well, it's almost four, so I'd better think about something to fix for dinner." She sighed. It had been an especially busy week for Mom, too. School started the next day and besides the regular work of maintaining a large family, there had been canning to do, school shopping to finish up, which meant going through all the kids clothes to see what they needed, and also being sure there were enough pencils, crayons, notebooks and erasers for everyone to take. Also, being almost eight months pregnant was making things alot harder to get done, and Mom was often exhausted at the end of the day.

"Don't worry about dinner, Grace," Dad said, pulling his shoes over and slipping them on before getting up from the couch. "I'll cook."

"What?" Mom said, surprise in her voice. Dad didn't come into the kitchen much, well, not to cook anyway. She wasn't sure what to think.

Dad chuckled. "I'll run into Sam's and get something for us to feed the crew," he said as he headed towards the door.

Theresa, who had been quietly listening as she played with an Etch-a-Sketch, jumped up, the toy forgotten. "Can I go with you, Dad?" She begged. As luck would have it she had been the only one in the room with her parents at the moment and this proved to be an opportunity for some time alone with Dad. A rarity in the Erb household.

"Sure, Linski," Dad said, using her pet name. Her name was Theresa Lynn, and Dad had a pet name for each kid. Linski was his version of Lynn.

Mom took a quick look at Theresa and decided she still looked good enough from church clean-up that morning to go into town and not be an embarrassment to mothers everywhere. She had actually stayed quite tidy. After lunch Rose and Sheila had offered her Sheila's Etch-a-Sketch to play with. They had been awfully nice about it, so she had accepted. She hadn't seen them since, but had joyfully played with the toy as she sat on the floor in the living room with Mom and Dad.

"Well, I'll just tidy up a bit before they get here," Mom said as Dad and Theresa headed towards the door. Theresa wondered what Mom would tidy. The house was neat from the Saturday cleaning and Mom looked as lovely as always. Maybe the baby in her tummy needed to be tidied.

It was a warm fall day. Dad opened Theresa's door and then closed it after she was in. He went around the front of the car, whistling, and got in. Soon they were on their way down the road, heading to town.

Spaeth's Grocery was on the edge of town. It was a yellow building that looked alot like a house, but the front room was a cute little grocery, with shelves stocked with lots of interesting things. Mostly the same things as the big grocery stores downtown had, but not nearly so much of each item. Sam Spaeth and his family lived behind the grocery. Theresa wondered if that was why he was open on Sundays while the big stores downtown were closed.

Dad greeted Sam as they entered the screen door. Sam was a shorter, roundish man with a friendly face. He always noticed children. Maybe because he had some of his own. "How are you today, young lady?" he asked Theresa now.

"Okay," Theresa replied, just a little bashful.

"Ready for school tomorrow?" he asked.

Theresa nodded yes.

"What grade will you be in?" Sam asked.

"First," Theresa said.

"My! You're growing up!" Sam said, as he smiled. Turning back to Dad he asked, "Anything I can help you with, Paul?"

"Just need a few things for supper," Dad replied. "Got any bologna or summer sausage?"

"Sure," said Sam, stepping from behind the counter and heading towards the back of the store. "I've got some in the cooler here. How much would you like?"

"Oh, couple pounds of each," Dad said, picking up some canned peach slices and pork and beans from the shelves. He sat them on the counter and added a big box of potato chips and some ice cream wafer cookies, in chocolate, strawberry and yellow. The pile grew larger as Dad put three loaves of light fluffy bread beside it and added a pail of ice cream. "Have you got any Colby cheese?" he asked Sam, when Sam returned with the meat wrapped in white paper.

"Sure do," said Sam. "How much do you want?"

"Probably a pound will do," Dad replied.

Sam went back to the cooler.

"Well, what else do you think we need?" Dad asked Theresa, as he waited by the counter for Sam.

Theresa thought the pile of food looked great. She couldn't think of anything to add, so she said, "I can't think of anything, Dad," feeling pretty grown-up that Dad would consult her on such important decisions as food purchasing. Dad walked around the store once more while waiting for Sam and the cheese. Theresa trailed him. He plucked two more items from the shelf and set them on the counter. Sam was back and begin to add the prices of things on the counter with a little adding type machine. Dad paid him and then Sam put the groceries into several big brown bags. He helped Dad carry them out to the car. Theresa carried the box of chips.

When they got home, the company hadn't arrived yet. Dad carried the groceries in and Mom went through them, seeing what Dad was going to "cook". Actually, Dad was done with his part of the "cooking". Now Mom would take over and put the meal together.

"Go upstairs and tell Diane I need her to come and help me," Mom told Theresa, as she folded the bags the groceries has come in and put them just inside the basement door. Theresa went up to relay the message to Diane. Diane was reading a book in her room. After telling her that Mom needed her help,

Theresa went into her own room, the one she shared with Rozanne and Sheila, to see if they were there. Nope. Theresa wondered what they were up to. She went back downstairs and picked up the Etch-a-Sketch again.

*****

Uncle David and Aunt Jean and their two sons, Mike and Dan, arrived soon after. Mike and Dan were around the ages of the three little girls, but of course, older than Theresa. No matter how you sliced it, it seemed she was always the youngest.

Sheila and Rozanne appeared out of nowhere when the company showed up. Dan went outside with the three girls, but Mike picked up a book and said he'd stay in. He loved to read. Dan loved the outdoors. It wasn't long before Theresa found out what Rozanne and Sheila had been up to that afternoon. They had found a garter snake. It was slim and long. Rozanne was so fond of God's creatures that she wanted to show it to Dan right off. The older girls had only touched it with a stick, but to the surprise of all three, Dan reached out and picked it up by the tail with his bare hands. He swung it around as the girls made a large arch away from him. My! He was brave! Rosy felt a little sorry for the snake and said, "Maybe we should put it down so it doesn't get dizzy."

Dan put it right back down on the ground. "Okay," he said. He was always nice to the girls and treated them with respect.

"D-I-N-N-E-R!" Diane called from the back step. The kids headed in to wash up for supper. Theresa couldn't wait to see how Dad's cooking would assemble into a meal. She smiled to herself thinking about Dad cooking. She'd noticed the last two items he'd added to the counter.

*****

Theresa decided that Dad was a pretty good cook. There was a huge platter with meat and cheese slices. Another with bread. A big bowl of chips and one of pork & beans sat on the table. Theresa looked around on the table until she spotted the black olives. They were one of the special treats Dad had picked up at the end of the shopping trip. The other was a bunch of bananas, which were sliced and added to the peach slices. Mom was just sitting the bowl on the table now. Everyone sat down. Theresa was sitting beside Sheila, with Mike next to her. Rozanne and Dan were across the table. After prayers the food was passed. When everyone had their plates filled, they began to eat. Theresa looked at Rozanne and noticed she was dipping up her pork & beans with a chip. Theresa figured if Rozanne could do it so could she. Wow. That was pretty good. Soon all the children were doing the same. It was a great way to eat chips-with bean dip! Rozanne was so clever!

Theresa sat back in her chair, eating the sandwich she had made by putting bologna between two slices of bread with butter. She looked around the table and enjoyed all the talk and laughter. Dan was telling Rozanne about snakes, Mike was telling Sheila about the paperback he'd just picked up when they arrived. He was half done reading it. He was a super fast reader. Theresa could hardly believe it. Dad and David were talking about farming. Mom and Jean were discussing the new baby's arrival with mention of a baby shower. Theresa wondered why you would shower a baby. She thought a bath would have to work because they didn't have a shower at their house.

She stuck an olive on her finger and ate it off. Then she scooped up the peaches with bananas. She loved bananas, but they didn't have them real often. They went further when you added them to peaches, Mom had said. After a while the table was partly cleared and Mom brought the pail of ice cream and Dad scooped it out. Strawberry. Wow! Was it good! Mom sent the ice cream wafers around. "Three each," she told her kids. That meant a chocolate, strawberry and yellow one per kid.

Theresa sat back again, full and content. She'd saved her yellow wafer for last. It was her favorite. As she broke it apart to eat the creamy center first, she caught Dad's eye and he winked at her. She smiled back around the cookie as if to tell him he had "cooked" a wonderful meal.

Aunt Jeannie & Uncle David

Erb Family Cookbook

Erb Family Cookbook

SALADS

BROCCOLI RAISIN SALAD — Kim

1-2 bunches broccoli, cut in small pieces
1 lb. bacon, fried, crumbled, drained
1 cup raisins
1 cup sunflower seed meats

Mix all together and toss with dressing:

1 cup Miracle Whip (NOT mayo)
1/2 cup sugar
2 Tbsp vinegar

COLESLAW — Mom

Grate one small head cabbage. Grate 1 carrot into cabbage. Chop 3-4 green onions, including some of the green (or you may just add chopped onion if green is not available). Mix. In a small bowl add 1/2 cup Miracle Whip, 1/4 cup sugar, 1/4 tsp salt, 1 Tbsp vinegar. Mix well. Slowly pour in ¼ cup milk until the dressing is smooth and all one consistency. You may need to add more sugar or vinegar depending on your preference. And maybe a little more milk if it's not the consistency you want. Pour over cabbage mixture and mix all together well. Refrigerate until ready to use.

CUCUMBER SLAW — Mom

Slice cukes. Sprinkle with salt. Let set 15 minutes or so. Drain and rinse well. Add sliced onions.

Make sauce of ¼ cup thick cream, 1 tsp sugar, and a tsp of vinegar. Mix well and pour over cukes and onions. Multiply as needed to cover cukes.

CHERRY FRUIT SALAD   Theresa

1 – 9 or 12 oz bowl cool whip
1 can cherry pie filling
1 can sweetened condensed milk
1 – 15 oz can drained crushed pineapple
1 – 11 oz can drained mandarin oranges
1-2 cups mini marshmallows
½ cup coconut
1 cup chopped pecans
Bananas, optional

Mix milk and cool whip. Add other ingredients. Add bananas right before serving. Makes a large bowl.

COOKIE SALAD   Theresa

2 cups buttermilk
2 pkgs instant vanilla pudding
12-16 oz Cool Whip
2 cans mandarin oranges, drained
1 pkg fudge striped cookies

Mix buttermilk and pudding with whisk. Fold in Cool Whip. Add mandarin oranges. Refrigerate until ready to serve. Break up cookies and stir in at serving time.

FRUIT PIZZA   Theresa

Crust:
½ cup margarine
1 cup flour
¼ cup powdered sugar
Mix well and pat out on ungreased pizza pan. Bake 350 degrees 10-15 minutes. Cool.
Second Layer:
1 – 8 oz cream cheese, softened
1/3 cup sugar
1 tsp vanilla
Mix and spread over cooled crust.
Third layer:
Fresh Fruit-blueberries, strawberries, raspberries, pineapple tidbits, kiwi, etc. Use desired amount and put in rings/rows on top of 2nd layer. Fourth layer: Glaze-2 Tbsp cornstarch, ½ cup sugar, juice from fruits and water to make 1 cup, and 1 tsp lemon juice. Cook until thick. Cool slightly. Pour over top of fruit. Chill. Serve the same day.

GLORIFIED RICE   Rozanne

1 cup rice
2 cups water
Milk
1 cup sugar
1 small can drained pineapple, crushed
½ bottle maraschino cherries with juice
8 oz Cool Whip

Cook rice in water until all is absorbed, then add 1 cup sugar and milk just to cover rice. Cook over low heat until thickened. Cool. Add drained pineapple, chopped maraschino cherries and ½ bottle of cherry juice. Fold in cool whip; chill well.

HOLIDAY CRANBERRY SALAD   Grandma Erb

1 pkg red jello
2/3 cup boiling water
½ cup pineapple juice
1 cup sugar
1 cup ground cranberries
1 cup ground apples with skins
1 cup crushed pineapple
½ cup white grapes
½ cup chopped nuts

HOT BEAN SALAD   Mom

1 15 oz can butter beans
1 15 oz can green beans
1 15 oz can green lima beans
1 15 oz can kidney beans
1 11 oz can baked beans
8 slices fried bacon, crumbled
1 cup brown sugar
1 onion, chopped
½ tsp garlic powder
1 tsp salt
½ cup vinegar
1 tsp dry mustard

Drain beans. Mix all together. Simmer 20 minutes at 350 degrees in an electric skillet or in oven.

MEXICAN SALAD   Sheila

Delicious apples
Avocados
¼ cup lemon juice
Fresh pineapple,
Oranges
Romaine lettuce, shredded
fresh strawberries
1/2 to 1/3 cup coconut
1 c. sugar
1/4 cup water
1 tsp grated lime rind
juice of 2 limes

Cut apples and avocados into wedges. Combine with lemon juice and toss to coat. Cut pineapple into cubes, slice oranges crosswise. Place lettuce on serving plate. Arrange apples, avocados, pineapples, oranges, and strawberries over lettuce. Sprinkle with coconut. Combine sugar, water, lime rind, and lime juice in small bowl; mix well. Pour over salad as dressing.

MEXICAN SALAD   Mom

Brown 1½ lbs. hamburger with chopped onion until done. Add ½ cup Western Dressing, ½ cup water and 1 Tbsp chili powder. Simmer 20 minutes. Then add 1 can (1# size) kidney beans and heat thoroughly. Place one head lettuce, torn in small pieces into large bowl. Add 1 pound grated longhorn cheese and 1 package Nacho Cheese Doritos, broken, to the lettuce. Mix in meat mixture. Serve immediately.

PEACH SALAD   Grandma Erb

1 can peach pie mix
1 can mandarin oranges
1 can pineapple chunks
1 can fruit cocktail
1 small jar red cherries (maraschino)

Drain all your fruits and add to the pie mix. Mix real good, put in fridge overnight. In the morning add cut bananas. Keeps real good and serves a lot.

POTATO SALAD   Mom

Boil potatoes with jackets (peelings) on. (Red are the best for potato salad.) Boil eggs. Cool both. Peel potatoes and cut into cubes. Peel eggs and cut into cubes. Add chopped onion, if desired. (Otherwise you can substitute onion powder in the dressing.) Mix approximately one cup Miracle Whip, 2 Tbsp sugar, 2 Tbsp. prepared mustard and 1 tsp salt. (May add onion powder to dressing now.) Mix well. Add about ¼ cup milk and mix until smooth. Pour over potatoes and eggs in bowl. Mix well. Cover and refrigerate until ready to serve. This is actually better if it is made ahead and sits a few hours before serving.

QUICK SALAD

12 oz cottage cheese
9 oz Cool Whip
15 oz can crushed drained pineapple
1 pint fresh strawberries, halved
1 – 3 oz strawberry jello

Mix all together.
Variation: Omit strawberries and use orange jello instead of strawberry jello.

SALAD   Aunt Jeannie

2 pkgs lemon jello
2 cups hot water
2 cups pineapple juice

Chill until slightly thickened. Whip and add:
1 cup crushed pineapple
1 cup cream, whipped
1 cup nuts
1 cup cottage cheese, small curd
Chill well.

TUNA MACARONI SALAD   Ruth Ann

1 pkg frozen peas
6 hard boiled eggs, diced
1 onion, diced
1 cup celery, diced
1 can tuna
Salt and pepper to taste
2 cups small shell macaroni
Miracle Whip

Cook macaroni until tender. Cool. Then add peas, onion, celery, tuna, eggs, salt and pepper. Add Miracle Whip-as much as you like.

VEGGIE PIZZA   Kim

2 pkgs crescent rolls
1/4 tsp dill weed
8 oz cream cheese
1/8 tsp garlic powder
6 Tbsp Miracle Whip

1/2 pkg Hidden Valley Ranch mix
4 cups chopped raw veggies (broccoli, carrots, celery, whatever)
4 oz. shredded cheddar cheese

Place the crescent rolls on baking sheet, spread out and pinched together to form flat crust (don't roll into crescent). Bake as per instructions; cool. Mix next 5 other ingredients together, except veggies and cheese; spread on cooled crust. Top with veggies, then with cheddar. Place under broiler JUST UNTIL CHEESE BEGINS TO MELT; then cut into squares.

VEGGIE PIZZA   **Theresa**

2 pkgs crescent rolls
16 oz sour cream
1 pkg dry ranch dip mix
your favorite raw veggies

Press crescent rolls out on jellyroll or large pizza pan. Bake until golden brown, approximately 8-10 minutes. Mix sour cream and dip mix. Spread ½ over cooled crust. Save other half for another use. Sprinkle chopped veggies on top. Chill until ready to serve.
I like to use broccoli, cauliflower, carrots, radishes, cukes, black olives and finely shredded cheddar cheese on mine.

WILD RICE SALAD   **Theresa**

1 cup wild rice, cooked
3 cups baked or boiled chicken breast, cubed
1 cup sliced water chestnuts
½ cup chopped green onion
2/3 to 1 cup Miracle Whip

½ cup cashews
1 cup green grapes

Mix all, except cashews, cover and refrigerate several hours. Add cashews at serving time.

BEST "HOUSE" SALAD DRESSING   Kim

1 cup mayo
1 cup Miracle Whip
1/4 cup grated Parmesan cheese
1/3 cup sugar

Mix all; refrigerate several hours before serving.

FRENCH DRESSING   Aunt Verda

½ cup oil
1 tsp onion
½ cup sugar
1 tsp celery seed
1 cup ketchup
Pinch of salt
3 Tbsp vinegar
2 Tbsp green pepper, cut fine

Beat oil and sugar together 5 minutes in blender; then add green pepper and onion, other ingredients last.

SOUPS

BROCCOLI CHEESE SOUP — Theresa

4 cups broccoli flowerets (fresh)
1 cup finely chopped celery
6 Tbsp minced onion
½ cup margarine
½ cup flour
4 cups milk
3 cups chicken broth
½ tsp celery salt
½ tsp pepper
1 ½ cup finely chopped ham
1 ½ cup shredded American cheese

Cook broccoli, celery & onion in small amount of water for 5 minutes or so. Drain and set aside. In another pan, melt margarine. Stir in flour. Gradually add milk and broth, stirring after each. Cook until smooth, stirring constantly. Add seasonings, broccoli and ham. Simmer 10 minutes, stirring frequently. Add cheese and stir until melted. Serve.

CHICKEN SOUP — Mom

Boil a cut up chicken, several stalks of celery, a couple of large carrots and 4 bouillon cubes in a large pot nearly full of water. Cook until meat is well done. Remove chicken, discard carrots and celery and strain broth. Remove skin and bones from chicken. Put broth back into pot. Add several stalks of chopped celery, 2-3 large carrots, chopped, and the chicken, cut in small pieces. Bring to a boil; cook until vegetables are tender, about 10 minutes. Add noodles and cook until done. *(Noodle recipe follows.)*

Erb Family Cookbook

HOMEMADE NOODLES   **Mom**

Eggs
Salt
Flour

The amount of noodles you want will determine how many eggs you use. 3 eggs will feed approximately 4-5 people. Mix eggs with fork. Add flour enough to make a stiff dough and sprinkle in salt as you work in the flour. When the dough is pretty much all in a ball, take it from the bowl and knead it on a flour covered counter until smooth. This should be a firm dough. Roll out on floured counter as thin as you can. Cut with knife in ½" strips about 6-8 inches long. Add to soup and cook.

Rozanne

CHICKEN WILD RICE SOUP   **Theresa**

5 cups water
2 chicken breasts
3 Tbsp chicken bouillon
2 celery, chopped

1 large carrot, chopped
3 level Tbsp cornstarch
2 cups ½ & ½
1 pkg Uncle Ben's Long Grain and Wild Rice

Cook chicken breasts in water with bouillon. Remove chicken from broth and cool. Then cut up and set aside. In broth, cook carrot, celery, the rice, and ½ the seasoning mix included with the rice, for about 30 minutes. Mix half and half and cornstarch, then add to broth. Stir until thickened. May need to add more milk at this time to get consistency you like. Then add chicken and heat through. Makes about 2 qts.

(When you are ready to use the remaining half pkg of seasoning, you will need about ¾ cup rice from your cupboard. I often use only white rice the 2nd time. You may also use a cut up chicken instead of the chicken breasts.)

CHILI Ruth Ann

2 lbs ground beef
2 large onions
½ large stalk of celery (leaves also)
4 cans hot chili beans
3 heaping Tbsp brown sugar
3 heaping Tbsp dried veggie flakes
1 large tsp chili powder
dash of garlic powder
2 qts tomato juice
salt and pepper to taste

Brown ground beef, onions, celery and add rest of ingredients. Simmer slowly for several hours.

ELEPHANT STEW Theresa via Diane

1 elephant
2 rabbits (optional)
Salt and pepper

Cut elephant into bite-sized pieces (takes about two months). Add brown gravy to cover. Cook about 4 weeks in a 450 degree oven. Serves 3800. For larger groups add 2 rabbits, but only if necessary. Most people don't like to find hares in their stew.
(Diane gave me this recipe when I was a young teenager. I thought it was so cute, I had to include it.)

POTATO SOUP Grandma Erb

Cook cubed potatoes with chopped onions until done. Drain most of the water off. Mash potatoes slightly, then add milk and cream. Heat through. Right before serving, tear up bread and float on top.

TACO SOUP   Theresa

1 lb hamburger
¼ cup chopped onion
2 pints canned tomatoes
16 oz tomato sauce
2 cups corn
1-16 oz can kidney beans
1 pkg taco seasoning

Brown hamburger with onion. Drain. Add other ingredients. Simmer ½ hour or more. Serve with corn chips, grated cheese and sour cream.

TOMATO SOUP WITH MACARONI   Mom

Cook ½ to 1 cup elbow macaroni according to box directions until done. Drain. Mix a can of Campbell's Tomato soup with 1 can of milk. Heat. Add macaroni and soup together and serve.

Theresa and Diane

VEGETABLES

BAKED BEANS Mom

Add some ketchup and brown sugar to pork & beans. Mix well and bake until hot. May add a dash of liquid smoke.

CREAMED BEANS

Cook green beans with onion slices until onions and beans are done. Drain juice from beans. Pour cream over beans until nearly covered. Heat gently until cream is warmed. Salt and serve.

CREAMED GARDEN VEGETABLES Mom

Cook potatoes, beans, peas, and carrots until done. (We usually cooked the veggies separate from each other.) Drain 2/3 of liquid off of potatoes. Drain all the liquid off of the other veggies. Mix two together. Add milk just to cover potatoes. Mix flour and milk together to make thickening. Heat veggies in milk until low boil. Add thickening and simmer until desired consistency. Add cream as it thickens. Add butter, salt and pepper, to taste.

CREAMED SPINACH Mom

Cook onions in butter until transparent. Add flour and brown, then add milk and cook until thickened. Cook spinach separately until done; drain. Add the two together. Heat through.
We liked this over mashed potatoes, too.

GREEN BEANS   Aunt Verda

4 slices bacon
3 Tbsp dry onion soup mix
1 Tbsp bacon drippings
1 Tbsp brown sugar
1 qt beans
¼ tsp salt
1 can tomato sauce

Cook bacon until crisp. Mix all together and bake at 350 degrees for 30 minutes.

OVEN BAKED MASHED POTATOES
Theresa

8-10 potatoes
1 - 8 oz cream cheese
1 cup sour cream
Salt & pepper
Boil and mash potatoes-don't add any liquid. Add remaining ingredients and beat well. Pour in a buttered casserole dish. Brush butter over top and sprinkle with seasoned salt. Bake uncovered for 45 minutes to one hour at 325-350 degrees. May cover with foil before baking and refrigerate overnight of freeze for later use. When ready to use, uncover and bake.

SCALLOPED CORN   Aunt Mabel

1 pkg frozen corn, thawed (1 pint)
2 eggs
1 Tbsp sugar
1 cup milk
½ lb American cheese, cubed

¾ cup crushed saltine crackers
Salt and pepper
Mix and bake in greased pan for about 1 hour or until golden and set.

SUNDAY FRIED POTATOES   Mom

Boil potatoes in skins until done. Cool. Peel and thinly slice. Place grease in hot pan and add potatoes. Spread out to evenly fill pan. Fry until potatoes began to brown on bottom. Flip and brown on other side. May need to add more oil. Salt and pepper.

Best if you don't put them in the frig after cooking. They get "watery" for frying. They keep several days at room temp.

Lois, Dale, Dad, & Mom

Diane's Christmas Taffy Pull

Theresa headed to the bathroom and spotted Diane in the bedroom across the hall. She was lying on her back on the bed; book in hand above her and a big bag of peanut M&Ms beside her. She ate a few now and then as she read.

Diane had graduated the year before and spent the last year away at college in Morris, MN. She had come home over the summer and gotten a job at the Nursing Home as a nurses' aide. Not sure if she wanted to continue college and having a full time job, she decided to take a year off from school and just work. She was thinking about finding a place of her own, but for now she was staying at home.

Theresa was envious. How she would <u>love</u> to be old enough to have a job with her own money to buy M&Ms and be able to spend a day lying in bed reading.

Diane spotted her. "Do you want some M&Ms?" she asked. Diane was always kind to her sisters. Theresa nodded and came in the room. Diane put her book face down on her stomach and lifted the bag. She poured some into Theresa's open hand.

"Is it still snowing?" Diane asked.

"It's kind of quitting, it looks like," Theresa said as she munched.

"Well," Diane said, "I talked to Rose and Sheila and asked them if they wanted to go caroling tonight. The old people in the nursing home love to have carolers come, so I told them I would try to drag my sisters out. We could go over to River Heights, too."

"That'd be fun," Theresa smiled. She felt so important when Diane did things with them.

"We'll go right after supper," Diane said. "When we get back we'll have a taffy pull."

"What's that?" Theresa asked.

"Taffy is a kind of a hard candy. You boil the ingredients and then pour it into a buttered pan. After it cools enough to handle it, but not too much, you take off pieces and pull it till it gets just right. Then you let it cool completely and break it into chunks to eat. I made it at a friend's house and they gave me the recipe. Taffy pulls were something young people used to do for get togethers, before there were movies and TV and such."

Theresa thought that sounded fun. She'd skip TV gladly to spend an evening with Diane.

*****

"It's pretty cold out there," Mom said. "Be sure you dress warm." A sad five year old Kimmy stood beside her, wishing she could go, but Mom had firmly said no.

The three girls were donning their outerwear and finding boots. They lived about half way between the Nursing Home and River Heights, which was a retirement home. River Heights was their first stop.

Dressed warm, with extra mittens in her pockets, Theresa was anxiously waiting to go. The girls were all in good spirits. Christmas was only a week away and the house smelled so good with all the treats that Mom was busy making. The favorite was her Buttercrunch. It was a toffee, cooked to perfection, and coated on both sides with chocolate and finely chopped nuts. Everyone loved it and Mom usually made several batches during the holidays.

Diane came down the stairs and laughed as she saw the three girls bundled up. "Are you ready to go?" she asked.

"Yep," said Rose for all of them.

"Be careful," said Mom, as they headed out. "And if it gets too cold come back. You can take the car if you need too."

"We'll be fine," Diane said. "Don't worry."

"That's what I'm supposed to do," said Mom, with a half hearted chuckle.

Outside the snow crunched under their boots. It was cold, but not unbearable. They were dressed warm. It was just a little over three blocks to River Heights. Trudging through the new snow kept them quite warm. As they talked among themselves, their breath came out in clouds of frosty white.

Theresa had been in River Heights several times. She had a little job helping an elderly couple, Mr. and Mrs. Lonny Shearer, by doing some light housework and preparing a simple dinner a couple of times a week. Mrs. Shearer was not feeling too well and Mr. Shearer was nearly blind. He wore thick glasses that made his eyes look big. They were both always happy to have Theresa come. She decided that they had to be sure to sing by their door.

Reaching River Heights, they went inside. As they began walking down the halls, they started to sing. First it was "Silent Night", then "Joy to the World." The three younger girls sang the melody and Diane sang a harmony line that made them sound really good. Because they were family, their voices blended together very nicely. They went up and down the halls singing more songs and then repeating some. They never stopped at any one place, just kept on moving. Some people would come out to see who was there and if it were the end of a song, they would clap. Everyone seemed to be filled with the holiday spirit.

After about ½ hour or so, the carolers left River Heights to head to the Nursing Home. They were pretty warm now, after being indoors all dressed in heavy winter wear.

"Anybody need to stop at home?" Diane asked, as they came to the block their house was on.

The answer "no" came from all three. As they walked they talked. Rozanne was in High School this year and she was talking about trying out as a cheerleader for the Wrestling Team. Paul wrestled on the Park Rapids Panther Team and they often went to his meets with Dad and Mom. But Mom didn't enjoy it much. She didn't like seeing her son getting roughed up. Paul wrestled the Heavy Weight Division and some of the opponents were really big compared to him..

Rozanne was also interested in gymnastics; she had led the girls in gymnastic maneuvers all her life, as far as Theresa could remember. Diane encouraged her to do both cheerleading and gymnastics. Sheila seemed interested in gymnastics, too. She asked Rose a lot of questions. Theresa couldn't wait until she was in High School.

There was a little park right beside the Nursing Home. Known as "Lindquist Park", it had only a few pieces of equipment. There were three swings hanging from a very high frame, some kind of a round metal jungle gym type piece, a merry-go-round, and the best slide in any of the local parks. It was very tall with lots of steps.

The girls looked at the park blanketed with snow and noticed how peaceful it looked. There was just a hint of light reaching it from the lights of the Nursing Home.

They slipped in the back door, where the employees entered. Theresa's glasses fogged up, as did the other girls. They all took them off and waited a few minutes for them to clear before going on in.

"We'll go down the halls that I work in," Diane said, "And then we'll go to the wing where the really ailing people are. They don't come out much, but they'll still like the music."

Again, as they walked and sang, Diane added the harmony to their music. The residents of the Home seemed to love their singing. When they got to the wing with the frailest and oldest people, Theresa noticed they just watched, but didn't say much. Many were in wheelchairs. A few walked along the hall. And some were already tucked into bed.

Diane stopped and talked to some of the other workers. She was having a couple of days off, and they talked a bit about the residents and how they were doing.

As they left, Diane said, "Let's go into the park and go down the slide. We'll be heading home next so if we get wet it won't matter too much."

The approval for this idea was unanimous. Who'd ever heard of playing in the playground in the dark of winter? That Diane came up with the best ideas, Theresa thought to herself. She was such fun!

The slide was great in the winter, even better than summer sliding. At the bottom you landed in the snow. They took turns and then Diane suggested they make snow angels. Something they hadn't done much since they were quite little on the farm was playing in the snow. Now nearly all teenagers (Theresa was 12 and two months) it was just as fun as when they were younger. They laughed and played and even threw a few snowballs. Pretty soon they were wet and getting cold.

"We'd better head home," Diane said. "We don't want to catch a chill before Christmas. Mom wouldn't let me take you all out again!' She laughed.

They trudged home as quickly as possible. They were starting to get pretty cold when they came in the back door.

"What happened to you?" Mom said when she saw them.

"We decided to play in the park!" Theresa exclaimed. "Diane is such fun!"

*****

Diane's taffy was cooking on the stove. She stood stirring it. The other girls and Kimmy were sitting at the round table having a cup of hot chocolate. They had removed all their wet clothes and put on their pajamas and robes. The warmth of the house after the cold outside, the taste of the hot chocolate in her mouth, and the sweet smell of the taffy cooking gave Theresa one of those moments where she felt utterly at peace with her family and the world. She was aware that her family was special. Things weren't always perfect in it, but she knew they shared something unique. Sometimes she squabbled with her sisters, but overall, she would have to say they were her dearest friends. She sipped her hot chocolate and her heart sent a silent "Thank You" to God for her family.

Diane poured the golden sugar mixture out on a pan. "It has to cool a little bit before we can pull it," she said, "but not too long. It will seem hot but you just keep pulling and it will cool off."

After a short wait, (too short Theresa thought) Diane took a knife and cut off a chunk. She buttered her fingers and then began to pull the candy out into foot long pieces. Then she would refold it and pull again. Sometimes the long silky threads were as much as a foot and a half in length. She did it quickly. Theresa knew why after she took her piece. It was hot! All five girls stood in the kitchen pulling and laughing. As they lay the long ropes of hardened taffy down, they would cool. After one rope was cool enough, Diane broke it into bite sized pieces and everyone sampled. It was wonderful!

Mom sat at the table addressing the last few Christmas cards she had left. Dad was at work. He was the night jailer over at the Sheriff's Office. Paul had gone out on a date.

The girls cleaned up the kitchen when they were done and took out the Carom board. It was a game that was played often in their home. Grandma Erb and Dad were the hardest to beat, but the kids all loved to try. A little practice was always a good idea whenever they had a chance. The wooden board was about three feet square with little net "pockets" on the four rounded corners. The center looked like a checker board. Caroms were little round plastic rings and the object of the game was to shoot all your colored rings into the pockets before your opponent did. Half were green and half were red. There was one black one, worth more points than the rest. All the pieces (about 12 of each color) were put in the center along with the black one and then you took your white shooter and snapped it into the center to break them all apart. From there on you worked at getting your color in by using your shooter in various shots. The four oldest girls played and Kimmy went happily around the table watching each player. She got terribly excited when the black one went in and the player couldn't save it (putting one of their own color in immediately or the black one had to come out). After awhile the girls put the game away and all went into the living room to lie under the Christmas tree and play the game they had grown up with. Each person lay on the floor under the tree and looked up at the lights through the branches. They would then take turns guessing which ornament each was looking at, based on certain clues, like, "I see something round and shiny." This was a game they had made up as children and still loved.

     Theresa lay under the tree, looking up at the decorations and loving every moment of the holiday season. Christmas meant so much to her. She thought about her parents. How much they loved her. She never ever questioned that. She just knew it, like she knew of God's love for her. And she thought about her siblings; each special in their own way and each special in her heart. Diane, thoughtful and kind, taking her time to spend with her sisters; Paul, who was always busy tinkering at something, but still found time to make them laugh; Rozanne, her humor always lightened any situation and made life fun; Sheila, quiet and gentle, drawing the good out of everyone, and little Kimmy, cuter than a bug and so happy and full of life. Christmas encompassed the extended family; her wonderful grandparents and the many aunts, uncles, and cousins. She thought of the caroling they had done and all the goodies that waited. She thought of the gifts that were beginning to show up under the tree. All of these memories brought a warmth of gratitude to Theresa's heart.

But Christmas was more than all of those things that passed through her thoughts. Most of all it was a time to remember the birth of God's Son, Jesus, who loved her so much He had died on the cross for her. She thought about that sweet little Baby and the suffering He would do just for her. And she felt such deep gratitude that a tear slipped out and blurred the lights in the tree above her….

Erb Family Cookbook

Theresa, Diane, Kimberly, Rozanne, Sheila

Diane, Theresa, Kimberly, Sheila, Rozanne

Family

In many ways so different
But in fact one of the same.
What binds us all together
Goes far beyond our name.

To find such perfect union
Is certainly given from above.
What we share in joy and sorrow
Only strengthens our great love.

May we grow beyond our measure
To reach to those with less,
And somehow give to them a share
Of with what we have been blest.

And always being thankful
For the ones we hold so dear;
Remembering to tell them
Every day throughout the year.

For even through eternity
We're bound to one another,
Because family lives on and on
Within the hearts of others.

~tlhenderson

APPETIZERS
Buffalo Wings..16
Cheese Ball...16
Devilled Eggs..16
Pickle Roll-Ups...17
Wingies..17

BARS
Brownies...18
Date Bars..18
Date & Orange Slice Bars...19
German Chocolate Caramel Bars..............................20
Graham Crackers Bars..20
Lemon Bars..20
Mixed Nut Bars..21
Peanut Butter Bars..21
Pumpkin Bars..22
Raisin Bars...22
Raisin Bars...23
Rice Krispy Bars..38
Salted Nut Roll Bars...23
Seven Layer Bars...24
Sugarless Bars...24
Toffee Squares..25
Yummy Wheaties Bars...25

BEVERAGES
Hot Chocolate...32
Hot Chocolate...32

BREADS
Amish Pumpkin Bread..33

Banana Nut Bread..33
Banana Bread..34
Blueberry Muffins...35
Caramel Rolls...36
Donuts..36
Easy Caramel Rolls..36
Light & Airy Buns..37
Overnight Buns..37
Peaches & Cream Muffins....................................38
Roll Dough...39
Rye Bread...40
Strawberry Butter...40

BREAKFAST DISHES
Best Buttermilk Pancakes....................................41
Grandma's Easter Eggs..41
Liver Sausage...42
Liverwurst..43
Mom's Pancakes with Maple Syrup.....................44
Oatmeal Pancakes..44
Omelettes...45
Oven Breakfast...45

CAKES & FROSTINGS
Apple Chunk Cake...48
Applesauce Cake..48
Applesauce Cake..49
Applesauce Cake..49
Banana Cake..50
Banana Nut Cake..50
Birthday Cake w/Frosting....................................51
Chocolate Cake..52
Cold Water Devil's Food Cake.............................52

Erb Family Cookbook

Easy Chocolate Cake......53
Fruit Cake......53
Fruit Cake......54
German Sweet Chocolate Cake......54
Hot Milk Cake......56
Oatmeal Cake......57
Peanut Cake......57
Prune Cake......58
Sour Cream Burnt Sugar Cake......58
Wacky Cake......59
White Cake......59

Frostings:
Banana Cake Frosting......59
Coconut-Pecan Filling and Frosting......60
Double Boiler Frosting ("7 Minute Icing")......60
Easy Penuche Frosting......61
Lucille's Frosting......61
Sour Cream Burnt Sugar Cake Frosting......61

CANDY
Almond Bark......66
Almond Bark Candy......66
Black Walnut Brittle......66
Best Ever Popcorn Balls......67
Caramels......67
Caramels......67
Caramels......68
Christmas Buttercrunch......68
Corn Flake Candy......69
Divinity......70
Never Fail Fudge......70
Maple Fudge......71

Peanut Brittle...71
Popcorn Balls..72
Potato Candy..72
Taffy..72
Sweetened Condensed Milk...73

CANNING & PRESERVING
Jams & Jellies:
Beet Jelly..74
Crabapple Butter...74
Rhubarb Jam..75
Rhubarb Jelly..75
Strawberry Jam..75
Triple Berry Jam..76
Pickles & Relishes:
Bread & Butter Pickles..76
Chunk Pickles..77
Crisp Sweet Pickles...77
Crispy Sweet Pickles...78
Hamburger Dills..78
Never Fail Dill Pickles...79
So Simple Sweet Pickles...79
Society Chip Pickles...79
Spiced Beets...80
Beet Relish..80
Corn Relish..81
Cucumber Carrot Relish..81
Misc.
Applesauce..81
Baked Cream Freezer Corn...82
Fruit Syrup for Pancakes...82
Homemade Tomato Soup...82
Pickled Fish...82

V-8 Tomato Juice...83

COOKIES
Amish Lebkucken..87
Applesauce Cookies..87
Banana Drops..88
Banana Oatmeal Cookies......................................88
Boiled Raisin Cookies..89
Brown Sugar Cookies..89
Buck Hill Cookies...90
Butterscotch Cookies..90
Caramel Cream Sandwich Cookies......................91
Chocolate Chip Cookies.......................................91
Chocolate Chip Cookies.......................................92
Chocolate Drop Cookies......................................92
Chocolate Gingersnaps..85
Chocolate Marshmallow Kisses...........................93
Christmas Sugar Shapes......................................93
Date Filled Cookies...94
Date Pinwheels..94
Delicious Cookies..95
Dorothy Yoder's Cookies......................................96
Easy Oatmeal Cookies..96
Farm House Cookies...97
Fruit Cookies..97
Gingies..98
Ginger Creams..98
Ginger Lace Cookies...99
Graham Cracker Cookies.....................................99
Gumdrop Cookies...99
Hawaiian Drop Cookies.......................................101
Ice Box Cookies..101
Ice Box Cookies..101

Mapeline Cookies..101
Million Dollar Cookies...101
Monster Cookies...102
No Bake Cookies...102
Oatmeal Cookies...103
Oatmeal Cookies...103
Old Fashioned Sugar Cookies................................104
Peanut Butter Cookies..104
Peanut Butter Cookies..104
Powdered Sugar Cookies.......................................105
Pumpkin Cookies...105
Ritz Crackers Cookies...106
Six in One Oatmeal Cookies..................................106
Snickerdoodles..107
Sparkling Gingersnaps..107
Sugar Cookies...108
Wagon Wheel Cookies..108
Washboard Cookies...109

DESSERTS
Almond Cheesecake...110
Apple Dumplings..111
Apple Pudding...111
Buster Bar Dessert..112
Fruit Cocktail Dessert..112
Ice Cream...113
Ice Cream...113
Lemon Refrigerator Dessert.................................114
Pecan Bar Dessert...114
Pumpkin Dessert...115
Pumpkin Pie Squares..115
Raspberry Dessert..116
Rhubarb Sauce...117

Sticky Chocolate Topping..117
Sweet Rice..117
White Chocolate Raspberry Cheesecake........................118
Yuletide Chocolate Dessert..119

MAIN COURSES
Bar-B-Q Hamburgers..124
Bean Hotdish..124
Chicken Breast Parmesan..124
Chicken Noodle Casserole..125
Dressing for Turkey or Chicken..125
Fried Chicken...126
HotDish..127
Marinated Chicken Breasts...127
Meatballs..128
Meat Loaf..128
Mexican Fiesta...129
Pennsylvania Scrapple..129
Sauerkraut Hotdish..130
Shrimp Creole..130
Spaghetti Sauce...131
Tacorettos..132
Tuna Sandwiches...132

PIES
Apple Pie...141
Banana Cream Pie..142
Butterscotch Raisin Pie...143
Chocolate Pie...143
French Apple Pie..144
Golden Pie Recipe..144
Fresh Blueberry Pie..145
Peaches & Cream Pie...145

Pecan Pie..146
Pumpkin Pie..146
Pumpkin Pie..147
Raisin Cream Pie..147
Raisin Pie...148
Raspberry Pie..148
Rhubarb Pie...149
Rhubarb Pie...149
Squash Pie...150
Strawberry Pie..150
Strawberry Pie..151
Mom's Pie Crust..151

SALADS
Broccoli Raisin Salad...161
Coleslaw..161
Cucumber Slaw...161
Cherry Fruit Salad..162
Cookie Salad...162
Fruit Pizza..163
Glorified Rice..163
Holiday Cranberry Salad..164
Hot Bean Salad...164
Mexican Salad (Sheila's)...165
Mexican Salad (Mom's)..165
Peach Salad..166
Potato Salad...166
Quick Salad..166
Salad...167
Tuna Macaroni Salad..167
Veggie Pizza...167
Veggie Pizza 168
Wild Rice Salad..168

Best "House" Salad Dressing..169
French Dressing..169

SOUPS
Broccoli Cheese Soup...170
Chicken Soup w/Homemade Noodles...............................170
Chicken Wild Rice Soup..171
Chili..173
Elephant Stew..173
Potato Soup...173
Taco Soup..174
Tomato Soup with Macaroni..174

VEGETABLES
Baked Beans..175
Creamed Beans..175
Creamed Garden Vegetables...175
Cream Spinach...175
Green Beans..176
Oven Baked Mashed Potatoes...176
Scalloped Corn...176
Sunday Fried Potatoes...177

Erb Family Cookbook

Special Note:

I asked my siblings to contribute some of their favorite recipes from present day. Following is that list. Each recipe is already in the cookbook's index for you to find easily. You'll notice I contributed the most. One of the privileges that comes with being the author! ~Theresa

Diane:
Oatmeal Pancakes
Hot Milk Cake
Gingies
Pecan Bar Dessert

Sue (Paul):
Sugarless Bars
Gumdrop Cookies
Chicken Breast Parmesan
Marinated Chicken Breasts
Shrimp Creole

Rozanne:
Hot Chocolate Mix
Easy Caramel Rolls
Peanut Brittle
Delicious Cookies
Pumpkin Dessert
White Chocolate Raspberry Cheesecake
Glorified Rice

Erb Family Cookbook

<u>Sheila:</u>
Yummy Wheaties Bars
Almond Cheesecake
Buster Bar Dessert
Fresh Blueberry Dessert
Squash Pie
Mexican Salad

<u>Theresa:</u>
Cheese Ball
Devilled Eggs
Pickle Roll-Ups
Wingies
Lemon Bars
Banana Bread
Light & Airy Buns
Peaches & Cream Muffins
Best Buttermilk Pancakes
Caramels
Triple Berry Jam
Applesauce
Baked Freezer Corn
Chocolate Chip Cookies
Almond Cheesecake
Ice Cream
Bean Hotdish
Meatballs
Peaches & Cream Pie
Raspberry Pie
Strawberry Pie
Cherry Fruit Salad
Cookie Salad
Fruit Pizza

Erb Family Cookbook

<u>Theresa, con't</u>
Veggie Pizza
Wild Rice Salad
Broccoli Cheese Soup
Chicken Wild Rice Soup
Taco Soup

<u>Kimberly:</u>
Buffalo Wings
Hot Chocolate Mix
Strawberry Butter
Oven Breakfast
Banana Cake w/ Frosting
Easy Chocolate Cake
Best Ever Popcorn Balls
Sweetened Condensed Milk
Broccoli Raisin Salad
Veggie Pizza
Best "House" Salad Dressing

Erb Family Cookbook

Erb Family Cookbook
Erb Family Tree

David and Anna (Greiser) Erb
(**Grandpa & Grandma Erb**) begat

1. Mabel (Gene Shipman) begat Ruth, Dean, Richard, Robert
(Rome Villiard) begat Merlyn, Shirley, Mary

2. Ruth (Vernon Wegman) begat George, Marilyn
(Charlie Yost)

3. Alice (Ezra Stutzman) begat, Sharon, John, Mary, Arla, Dan, DeeAnn
(Virgil Ott)

4. Ellen (Art Van Dyke)
(Clarence Cook) begat Doug, Debbie

5. David (Jeannie Forsberg) begat Mike, Dan

6. Paul ~ **Dad** (Grace Oswald ~ **Mom**) begat Diane, Paul, Rozanne, Sheila, Theresa, Kimberly
(Mary Krueger)

7. James (Verda Hoffman) begat Ron, LaVon, Nancy, Tim, Phillip, Rick

8. Anna (Earlis Miller) begat Bruce
(Duane Schmidt) begat Lisa

9. Mary Joanne

Erb Family Cookbook
Oswald Family Tree

Amos and Anna (Schneider) Oswald
(**Grandpa & Grandma Oswald**) begat

Dale (Lois Hoffman) begat Shirley, Dennis, Judy, Jerry, Gordon, Patrick, Kathy, Harley, Larry, Tim, Tom
(Gloria Vogt) begat Chris, Cory

Grace ~ **Mom** (Paul Erb ~ **Dad**) begat Diane, Paul, Rozanne, Sheila, Theresa, Kimberly

Made in the USA
Charleston, SC
01 August 2011